THE COOK'S COMPANION

Edited by Jo Swinnerton

A THINK BOOK FOR

ROBSON BOOKS

A cook, when I dine, seems to me a divine being, who from the depths of his kitchen rules the human race. One considers him as a minister of heaven, because his kitchen is a temple, in which his ovens are the altar.

Marc Antoine Desaugiers,
19th-century French poet

THINK
A Think Book
for Robson Books

First published in Great Britain in 2004 by
Robson Books
The Chrysalis Building, Bramley Road, London W10 6SP

An imprint of **Chrysalis** Books Group plc

Edited by Jo Swinnerton
The Companion team: Vicky Bamforth, Sarah Bove, James Collins,
Harry Glass, Rhiannon Guy, Annabel Holmes, Emma Jones,
Lou Millward Tait and Malcolm Tait

Think Publishing
The Pall Mall Deposit
124-128 Barlby Road, London W10 6BL
www.thinkpublishing.co.uk

The Soil Association
Registered charity number 206862
0117 914 2447
www.soilassociation.org

ISBN 1-86105-777-5

Printed and bound by Clays Ltd, Bungay, Suffolk NR35 1ED

Always take a good look at what you're about to eat. It's not so important to know what it is, but it's critical to know what it was.

Anon

WITH THANKS AND A BIG PIECE OF CAKE TO...

For their help, ideas, encouragement, fact-checking and the
loan of useful books:

Anna Crane, Kelly Ferguson, Katherine Lawrey,
Marie-Pierre Moine, Iain Swinnerton
and Tom de Pass of the Soil Association.

INTRODUCTION

There are some things in life that you simply need to know.

That scientists recommend the butter be one-seventeenth the thickness of the toast. That a Jerusalem artichoke is neither from Jerusalem nor an artichoke. That cannibals consider the French to be the most delicious and Spaniards barely edible. That to ask for a Duke of York for your Jack The Ripper in a cockney caff is to ask for a fork for your kipper. And that you can't hide a piece of broccoli in a glass of milk.

This little book is no flighty, dippy little fal-de-ral to amuse you in the loo, but a finely crafted, precisely researched, sharply written tomette that just happens to be full of the things you need to know.

You need to know what an anthropophagist eats. What it means to dine with Democritus. Why never to trust a dog to look after your food. That there will always be nine promising ingredients in the cupboard, but that in no combination will they actually make a meal. And that the trouble with eating Italian food is that five or six days later, you're hungry again.

The Cook's Companion transcends diet regimes, unnatural recipes and tyrannically fashionable ingredients. It is a well-stocked fridge for the mind, ready for leisurely feasting or fast midnight raids.

On a need-to-know basis, this book is more useful than Delia, more stimulating than Jamie and more tempting than Nigella. It has the answers to the questions you have never thought to ask. The perfect companion for people with a hunger for knowledge and a thirst for amusement, it does exactly what good food does: nourish, sustain, and make you feel better.

Jill Dupleix, The Times Cook

COOKING CONUNDRUMS

What famous concoction do these ingredients make? *Answer on page 153*

Golden Gloss hair shampoo

Toothpaste

Superfoam shaving soap

Vitamin-enriched face cream

Nail varnish

Hair remover

Dishworth's famous dandruff cure

Brillident for cleaning false teeth

Nevermore Ponking deodorant spray

Liquid paraffin

Helga's hairset

Flowers of turnip perfume

Pink plaster powder

Lipstick

Superwhite for automatic washing machines

Waxwell floor polish

Flea powder for dogs

Canary seed

Brown shoe polish

Bottle of gin

Tin of curry powder

Tin of mustard powder

Bottle of 'extra hot' chilli sauce

Tin of black peppercorns

Bottle of horseradish sauce

Powder for chickens with foul pest, hen gripe, sore beaks, gammy legs, cockerlitis, egg trouble, broodiness or loss of feathers

Pills for horses with hoarse throats

Medicine for cows, bulls and bullocks

Sheepdip

Pig pills

Engine oil

Anti-freeze

Grease

Dark brown gloss paint

QUOTE UNQUOTE

There are two things in life I like firm, and one of them is jelly.
MAE WEST, US actress

CULINARY LEGENDS

What **Eliza Acton** (1799-1859) really wanted to do was write poetry. But her publisher doubted he could sell a collection of poems by a woman, so he advised her to go away and write a good, sensible cookbook instead. The result was *Modern Cookery for Private Families* (1845) probably the first basic cookbook for the housewife, since cook books until then had been written for the trained chef with a full kitchen staff. Eliza spent years testing the recipes, which were well written and easy to understand, and for the first time ingredients were listed separately, rather than in the body of the recipe, which helped to make the book an immediate and long-lasting success.

THE DEEPER MEANING OF FOOD

In *The Meaning of Liff* and *The Deeper Meaning of Liff*, Douglas Adams and John Lloyd addressed the troubling problem that there are many everyday events in life for which there is no recognised word. And yet, there are plenty of place names hanging about the countryside that seemed to describe them perfectly. So the two were brought together, and the result is pure absurdist joy.

Abinger (n.) One who washes up everything except the frying-pan, the cheese-grater and the saucepan which the chocolate sauce has been made in.

Aigburth (n.) Any piece of readily identifiable anatomy found among cooked meat.

Beccles (n.) The small bone buttons placed in bacon sandwiches by unemployed guerrilla dentists.

Berkhamsted (n.) The massive three-course mid morning blow-out enjoyed by a dieter who has already done his or her slimming duty by having a teaspoonful of cottage cheese for breakfast.

Cannock chase (n.) In any box of After Eight Mints, there is always a large number of empty envelopes and no more than four or five actual mints. The cannock chase is the process by which, no matter which part of the box you insert your fingers into, or how often, you will always extract most of the empty sachets before pinning down an actual mint, or 'cannock'.

Chimbote (n.) A newly fashionable ethnic stew, which however much everyone raves about it, seems to you to have rather a lot of fish-heads in it.

Cloates point (n.) The precise instant at which scrambled eggs are ready.

Cong (n.) Strange-shaped metal utensil found at the back of the saucepan cupboard. Many authorities believe that congs provide conclusive proof of the existence of a now-extinct form of a yellow vegetable which the Victorians used to boil mercilessly.

Corstorphine (n.) A very short peremptory service held in monasteries prior to teatime to offer thanks for the benediction of digestive biscuits.

Cresbard (n.) The light working lunch that Anne Hathaway used to prepare for her husband.

Cromarty (n.) The brittle sludge which clings to the top of ketchup bottles and plastic tomatoes in nasty cafes.

Darenth (n.) Measure = 0.0000176mg. Defined as that amount of margarine capable of covering one hundred slices of bread to the depth of one molecule. This is the legal maximum allowed in sandwich bars in Greater London.

Eriboll (n.) A brown bubble of cheese containing gaseous matter which grows on Welsh Rarebit.

Fraddam (n.) The small awkward-shaped piece of cheese which remains after grating a large regular-shaped piece of cheese, and which enables you to grate your fingers.

Goosnargh (n.) Something left over from preparing or eating a meal, which you store in the fridge, despite the fact that you know full well that you will never ever use it.

Gruids (n.) The only bits of an animal left after even the people who make sausage rolls have been at it.

Naples (pl.n.) The tiny depression in a piece of Ryvita.

Papple (v.) To do what babies do to soup with their spoons.

Peoria (n.) The fear of peeling too many potatoes.

Pott Shrigley (n.) The dried remains of a week-old casserole, eaten when extremely drunk at 2am.

Symond's Yat (n.) The little spoonful inside the lid of a recently opened boiled egg.

Throcking (v.) The action of continually pushing down the lever on a pop-up toaster in the hope that you will thereby get it to understand that you want it to toast something.

FILMS FOR FOODIES

American Pie
The Apple
Attack of the Killer Tomatoes
Bread and Roses
Candyman
Chocolat
Coffee and Cigarettes
Cookie
Days of Wine and Roses
Fortune Cookie
The Grapes of Wrath
The Honeytrap
*M*A*S*H*
Mystic Pizza
The Silence of the Lambs
Spiceworld
Tea with Mussolini

QUOTE UNQUOTE

There is no light so perfect as that which shines from an open fridge door at 2am.
NIGEL SLATER, food writer

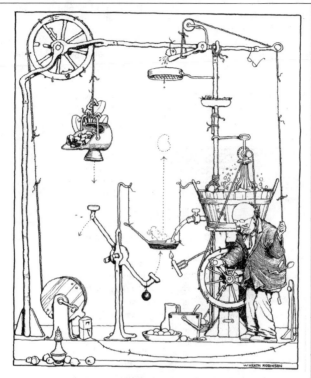

Professor Branestawm's Pancake Machine
illustrated by William Heath Robinson

'Here are the flour bin, the egg receptacle, the milk churn, and
the sugar canister and the lemon squisher... This is the pancake
pan, and this is the thickening regulator, by means of which you
can have pancakes any thickness you like. Here is the centrifugal
tossing gear with adjustable self-changing height regulator, and
my own patent device for calculating the number of tosses
required for pancakes of different thicknesses.'
'Will it go wrong?'
'Certainly not.'

Norman Hunter,
The Incredible Adventures of Professor Branestawm

LITERARY FEASTS

My memories of tea will have to be assembled without the help of Mipsie, for the whole subject brings her such nostalgia for Rumpelmeyer's in the Rue de Rivoli – the only place where tea has ever given her real pleasure, otherwise, she says it is a cheap meal – that I hesitate to re-open old wounds. The famous *salle de thé* holds a special romance for her, for it was there that a Russian Prince, after taking her to tea every day for a fortnight, shot himself at her feet because he couldn't pay the bill. 'Ah, Blanche,' poor Mipsie said when we were discussing it this morning, 'we shall never see those days again. Nowadays nobody has enough money to do what they can't afford.'

Mary Dunn, *Lady Addle at Home*

SPOILT FOR CHOICE

This is just a handful of the thousands of varieties of English apple that exist. So if all you get at your local store is Golden Delicious, make friends with your local fruit farm:

Blenheim Orange	Histon Favourite
Christmas Pearmain	King of the Pippins
Cornish Gillflower	Michaelmas Red
Crimson Beauty of Bath	May Queen
Chelmsford Wonder	Merton Prolific
Chivers Delight	Nanny
Cornish Aromatic	Nutmeg Pipping
Crawley Beauty	Peasgood's Nonsuch
Easter Orange	Pig's Nose Pippin
Falstaff	Rosemary Russet
Greensleeves	St Edmund's Russet
Hawthornden	Tydeman's Late Orange
Hoary Morning	Worcester Pearmain

STRANGE DIETS

A Dutchman who has eaten pigeon food for three meals a day for the last 11 years claims it could be the answer to world famine.

Gerben Hoeksma, 58, from Veendam, says his meals are nutritious, filling and cost him next to nothing. He told *Dagblad van het Noorden*: 'I first let the food soak in water for a night and then cook it the next day to get it softer.

'It has all the substances a man needs daily. Maybe it would be good food for the people in Africa. Since I started to eat pigeon food I never felt so good. I've never been sick in my life.'

LAST SUPPERS

In an article for *Observer Food Monthly*, when asked what their last suppers on earth would consist of, Raymond Blanc chose floating islands (meringues floating in a thin custard); Gordon Ramsay chose roasted sea bass with crushed new potatoes; Gary Rhodes asked for braised oxtail; Giorgio Locatelli preferred rabbit with Parma ham and polenta; and Michel Roux Jr would bow out with rabbit terrine cooked in Chablis with grain mustard.

REASONS TO EAT MORE CHOCOLATE

Needless to say, many of these things are found in foods other than chocolate without the high levels of sugar and saturated fat. But only a dull person would worry about that.

- Chocolate is high in antioxidants, natural chemicals that help to protect against diseases such as cancer and heart disease. It has nearly twice the antioxidants found in red wine and three times the amount found in green tea
- It is high in flavonoids, which can raise levels of 'good' cholesterol
- It reduces the risk of blood clotting
- It protects against stress on the heart
- It relaxes blood vessels, having a similar effect to mild aspirin and a better effect than red wine
- It contains iron and magnesium
- It contains caffeine, to stimulate
- It contains phenylethylamine, a 'feelgood' chemical that cheers you up

THE COST OF LIVING

We all complain about inflation, but how much has your bread and butter really gone up by?

	1952	1977	2004
White bread	6d	22p	60p
Butter lb	2/6d	54p	£1.54
Beef sirloin lb	2/6d	£1.41	£4.98
Back bacon lb	3/9d	95p	£2.82
Tea 1/4lb	11d	29p	69p (125g)
Granulated sugar 2lb ..	1/-	26.5p	57p
Eggs (doz)	5/3d	53p	£1.55
Potatoes (lb)	2d	4p	45p
Apples (lb)...................	6d	24p	68p
Pint of beer	1/3d	26.5p	£2

COOKS IN BOOKS

Whenever I have nothing better to do, I roast a chicken. On average, I have nothing better to do about twice a week. That comes to a thousand chickens since 1990, over two million calories in all. I'll roast a chicken in the afternoon even when I'm not hungry and have plenty of food in the fridge and a reservation for dinner. It's like a hobby.

I go through phases. By now I must have tried every conceivable variation, every pairing of temperature and time, trussing the chicken or leaving it loose, basting or not – with water, broth or butter, hot or cold. For months I will lay the little birds on their sides, then abruptly shift to the breast-up or breast-down school of thought. I have rubbed them first with herbs, spices, oil or butter, or left them plain, and slid truffles under the skin. I have browned them first on top of the stove before popping them in the oven, or used a rack, or a little wire tower. I have tried free-range, organic, Amish, kosher, and supermarket birds, one pound, three pounds or five pounds each. I have stuffed them with two lemons. You name it.

The great Brillat-Savarin declared: 'We can learn to be cooks, but we must be born knowing how to roast.' I often lie awake nights worrying about whether I was born to roast. It can be total agony.

Jeffrey Steingarten, *It Must've Been Something I Ate*

FIVE FATAL MEALS

In 1985, *The Lancet* reported the case of a 23-year-old model who died after eating 1lb liver, 2lbs kidney, 0.5lb steak, 1lb cheese, two eggs, two slices of bread, one cauliflower, 10 peaches, four pears, two apples, four bananas, 2lbs each of plums, carrots and grapes and two glasses of milk.

Alexander the Great died aged 32 after a prolonged bout of eating and drinking.

The day Abensee death camp was liberated, the liberating soldiers took pity on the starving prisoners and fed them pork and beans. Tragically the survivors' bodies couldn't handle the solid food, and many died while eating their first meal of freedom.

Mama Cass of fab Sixties group the Mamas and the Papas died eating a ham sandwich, though it was a heart attack, not the sandwich, that killed her.

Charles Morris Mount, who designed the McDonald's in New York's Times Square, died aged 60 at his home in Mattituck, New York in December 2002. He had a heart attack while eating breakfast. The newspaper reports did not record what he was eating.

FOOD FIGHTS

The largest ever recorded custard-pie fight took place on 11 April, 2000, at the Millennium Dome in London, when 3,312 custard pies were thrown in three minutes by 20 people.

GOOD FOOD FACTS

Fruit is one of nature's best medicines, and provides a tasty solution to lots of little problems. The traditional remedies that follow make use of the fact that many fruits are anti-bacterial and anti-viral, high in antioxidant vitamins (especially if they're organic) and rich in soluble fibre. Any **citrus fruits** will help speed the end of a **cold**, thanks to their anti-bacterial properties and high levels of vitamin C; **blackcurrants** are very good too. To soothe **coughs** and **colds**, drink **lemon** or **lime** juice mixed with hot water and honey. For **sore throats**, gargle with **lemon** juice mixed half and half with hot water (this makes a good homemade **mouthwash**, too), or sip homemade hot **blackcurrant** juice, made with blackcurrants, hot water and honey. For **diarrhoea**, eat **apples** or **pears**, **blackberries**, **raspberries** or **blackcurrants** – but eat in moderation or you'll make the situation worse. For **constipation**, an apple **grated** and left to go brown, then mixed with a little honey, is extremely effective. This is also an excellent remedy for an **upset stomach**, especially if you've been sick. Dried **apricots** and **peaches**, soaked in a little hot water will also help **constipation**, as will **melons**, **gooseberries** and **stewed rhubarb** (and plenty of **water**). For **cystitis** or urinary infections, eat raw **blueberries** or drink a glass of **cranberry juice** every day – both are powerfully anti-bacterial. For pus-filled **spots** or **cold sores**, apply neat **lime** or **lemon** juice with a cotton bud, as long as the skin is unbroken.

MONKEY'S BANQUET

The annual monkey banquet takes place in Lop Buri, a small town about 50 miles from Bangkok. But this is no euphemistic feast; the guests really are monkeys. The organiser, Yonguth Kijwattananuson, says that monkeys have added character and colour to the town and are consequently honoured once a year. Gourmet chefs are drafted in to prepare a feast of vegetarian delicacies, which are duly presented to the pampered primates. The ensuing food fight and general lack of any sort of table manners is generally considered as part of the fun by the mainly Buddhist locals and curious tourists.

GOOD ENOUGH TO EAT

Francis Bacon, painter (1909–1992)
Kevin Bacon, actor (1958–)
Chet Baker, US jazz trumpet player (1929–88)
Dame Janet Baker, opera singer (1933–)
Josephine Baker, French entertainer (1906–75)
Halle Berry, actor (1966–)
Jonathan Cake, actor (1967–)
Jasper Carrot, comedian (1945–)
Hamilton Fish, US politician (1808–93)
Elizabeth Fry, prison reformer (1780–1845)
Lady Caroline Lamb, writer and Byron's lover (1785–1828)
Charles Lamb, essayist and poet (1775–1835)
Jack Lemmon, actor (1925–2001)
Meatloaf, singer (1947–)
Jelly Roll Morton, jazz player (1890–1941)
Captain Lawrence Edward Grace Oates, explorer (1880–1912)
Sir Peter Neville Luard Pears, British tenor (1910–1986)
Alan Sugar, founder of Amstrad (1947–)

HEAD COOK

The word 'lady' means 'bread-maker' or 'kneader of dough' from the old English *hlaefdige*. It was not literal, but was supposed simply to refer to the female head of the household. Similarly, the word 'lord' comes from *hlaford*, meaning 'keeper of bread'.

THE TRUTH ABOUT JACK HORNER

Little Jack Horner
Sat in a corner,
Eating a Christmas pie;
He put in his thumb, and pulled out a plum,
And said, 'What a good boy am I!'

This nursery rhyme was said to refer to Jack Horner who was steward to the last abbot of Glastonbury, Abbot Whiting. During the dissolution of the monasteries, Abbot Whiting sent Horner to see Henry VIII with a large pie as a Christmas present. When the King examined his present, he found that it contained the deeds of 12 Somerset manors, intended as a bribe to the King to spare the monastery. The plum that Jack pulled out is thought to refer to the deeds to the Manor of Mells, which Horner kept for himself. His ancestors dispute the story, but a Thomas Horner did reside at Mells soon after the monasteries were dissolved.

COOKS IN BOOKS

While other cookery has room for error and a freehand style, it is important to measure carefully in baking... to be thorough in your folding, creaming and measuring... and to line your baking pans carefully and butter them, when directed, as thoroughly as *Last Tango in Paris*. It is also important to remember, for your own self-worth, that even the most experienced bakers have off days and that fruit inexplicably sinks in fruit cakes.

Clarissa Dickson-Wright, *Cooking with the Two Fat Ladies*

OLD PICTURE, NEW CAPTION

That oyster ragout is the business, thought George, as Isabel's inhibitions melted like warm butter on a plate of asparagus

EAT YOUR GREENS

In 2002, a first-year university student, overwhelmed with excitement at the size of his student loan, spent virtually all the money on an electric guitar within days of starting his course. Too ashamed to own up to his parents, he hit on the idea of feeding himself for the rest of the term with a catering-size pack of oatmeal. He was admitted to hospital over the Christmas holidays with malnutrition.

In 1912, Wilbur Scoville, an American chemist, devised a method to measure the hotness of chilli peppers. The Scoville Organoleptic Test involved blending pure ground chillies with a sugar and water solution, which was sipped by a panel of testers. The solutions were increasingly diluted until they no longer burned the mouth. A number was then assigned to that chilli pepper, based on how much it needed to be diluted before the tester could taste no heat.

Despite the Scoville testers' devotion to their task, the scale has been widely criticised, and alternative tests and scales have been devised, including the High-Performance Liquid Chromatography (HPLC) test, and the Gillett method. Nevertheless, the Scoville method has stood the test of time, and still offers a reliable guide – or perhaps a warning – to what you are about to receive. However, as individual types of pepper can vary from mild to hot, it can only ever be a guide. So chew carefully.

0-100: includes most sweet peppers
500-1000: includes New Mexican peppers
1000-1500: includes Espanola peppers
1000-2000: includes Ancho and Pasilla peppers
1000-2500: includes Cascabel and Cherry peppers
2500-5000: includes Jalapeno and Mirasol peppers
5000-15,000: includes Serrano peppers
15,000-30,000: includes de Arbol peppers
30,000-50,000: includes Cayenne and Tabasco peppers
50,000-100,000: includes Chiltepin peppers
100,000-350,000: includes Scotch Bonnet and Thai peppers
200,000-300,000: includes Habanero peppers
16,000,000: the heat level of pure capsaicin, the substance that gives peppers their heat. The heat is created by capsaicin, which is found not in the seeds, but at the point where the seed is attached to the white membrane inside the pepper.

The hottest chilli pepper in the world is currently believed to be the Red Savina Habanero pepper, rated at 577,000 Scoville units.

While chilli peppers may be edible, any food that comes with a warning (this one is from *Larousse Gastronomique*) should be treated with great respect: 'Try chillies and their products sparingly at first until acquainted with their flavour. The seeds inside a chilli are extremely hot and should be removed unless a fiery result is required. Capsaicin…is a severe irritant which can burn the skin, particularly delicate areas around the eyes and nails or any cuts. Always wash your hands thoroughly after preparing chillies and avoid touching your eyes; alternatively use disposable plastic gloves to prepare chillies.'

CHOCOLATE HISTORY

How old is your favourite bar of chocolate?

	Date first sold in the UK
Fry's Chocolate Cream	1866
Cadbury's Dairy Milk	1905
Cadbury's Bournville	1908
Cadbury's Milk Tray	1915
Cadbury's Flake	1920
Terry's Neapolitan	1922
Terry's 1767 Bitter Bar	1923
Cadbury's Creme Egg	1923
Fry's Turkish Delight	1924
Cadbury's Fruit & Nut	1928
Cadbury's Crunchie	1929
Maya Gold Fairtrade organic chocolate	1994

QUOTE UNQUOTE

Last night we went to a Chinese dinner at six and a French dinner at nine, and I can feel the sharks' fins navigating unhappily in the Burgundy.
PETER FLEMING, journalist and travel writer

FOOD FOR THOUGHT

World War II showed the need for Britain to have greater self-sufficiency when it came to growing its own food. It also encouraged the development and production of chemicals for weapons and explosives. The war over, the chemical-producing companies lobbied for the greater use of chemicals in agriculture, given that they had quite a lot left over.

Although farmers resisted at first, the *Agriculture Act of 1947* paid out generous subsidies on bags of fertilisers, encouraging farmers to rely more on chemical aids. Yield increased, but soil quality decreased, requiring more chemicals to be ploughed into the land. In the chemically fertilised soil, plants became more prone to insect and fungal attacks, and weeds grew more rapidly. These were treated with pesticides and herbicides.

In 1974, subsidies on fertilisers were dropped, but crops themselves were subsidised, meaning that farmers received a guaranteed price regardless of demand. Too much food was produced, so much of the surplus was exported to developing countries, undercutting the local farmers. Many of them went out of business and moved to urban centres in search of work, where Western aid in the form of cheap bread and milk helped them to survive. Today, some food surpluses are still sold overseas where they are not needed.

If you're a little fuzzy on those hygiene rules, here are six tips for a safer kitchen:

• Check your fridge temperature with a thermometer. The coldest part of the fridge should measure no more than 5°C. Defrost regularly – iced-up fridges don't stay cold as easily.

• Wash hands after handling raw foods and before touching other foods and utensils. Keep raw foods separate from cooked and ready-to-eat food, particularly raw meat and fish. Don't put cooked food on a plate that has previously held raw foods. Use separate chopping boards for raw and cooked foods.

• Thaw food by placing it on the bottom shelf of the fridge in a container to catch any juices. These juices can be contaminated, so wash the dish (and your hands) after handling. Thaw food in a microwave oven only if you're going to cook it straight away.

• Never refreeze food once it has been thawed. Once it has begun to thaw, it's too late to refreeze it. This also means that if you make, for example, a chicken casserole with frozen chicken, you can't freeze the leftovers.

• Don't put hot food directly into the fridge or freezer – let it cool first, or it will heat up the entire fridge. Eat leftovers within two days.

• Never reheat foods more than once. However tempting they look.

TEN FOODS TO FOOL YOU

Bombay duck is a northern Indian fish dish
Glamorgan sausages are sausage-shaped,
but made with cheese
A **Jerusalem artichoke** is neither from Jerusalem nor an
artichoke. It's an edible tuber from North America
A **peanut** is not a nut, it's a legume
Mock turtle soup is made with calf's head, beef and veal
A **Salisbury steak** is a hamburger
American coffee cake is a cake, but may not contain coffee;
it refers to any cake made to be eaten with a cup of coffee
Poor man's caviar is made of aubergines
Scotch woodcock is anchovies and eggs on toast
Boston crab is a wrestling manoeuvre

LITERARY FEASTS

Breakfast itself – not later than eight o'clock – ought in rigid training to consist of plain biscuit (not bread), broiled beef steaks or mutton chops, under-done, without any fat, and half a pint of bottled ale – the genuine Scots ale is the best. Our fair readers will not demur at this, when they are told that this was the regular breakfast of Queen Elizabeth and Lady Jane Grey. But should it be found too strong fare at the commencement, we permit, instead of the ale, one small breakfast cup – not more – of good strong black tea or coffee – weak tea or coffee is always bad for the nerves as well as the complexion.

Dr Kitchener, *The Cook's Oracle*, 1820

COOKING CONUNDRUMS

Who insulted whom by calling him a Banbury cheese?
Answer on page 153

COOKING TERMS REDEFINED

An anonymous posting on the internet, and a small work of genius:

Calorie – basic measure of the amount of rationalisation offered by the average individual prior to taking a second helping of a particular food.

Frying pan – standard instrument of destruction for eggs, pancakes, and various vegetable matter. Remains may be removed from surface with diluted solution of sulphuric acid.

Microwave oven – space-age kitchen appliance that uses the principle of radar to locate and immediately destroy any food placed within the cooking compartment.

Oven – compact home incinerator used for disposing of bulky pieces of meat and poultry.

Preheat – to turn on the heat in an oven for a period of time before cooking a dish, so that the fingers may be burned when the food is put in, as well as when it is removed.

Porridge – thick oatmeal rarely found on breakfast tables since children were granted the right to sue their parents. The name is an amalgamation of the words 'putrid', 'horrid', and 'sludge'.

Recipe – a series of step-by-step instructions for preparing ingredients you forgot to buy, in utensils you don't own, to make a dish the dog won't eat.

Tongue – a variety of meat, rarely served because it clearly crosses the line between a cut of beef and a piece of dead cow.

Yogurt – semi-solid dairy product made from partially evaporated and fermented milk. Yogurt is one of only three foods that taste exactly the same as they sound. The other two are goulash and squid.

A SPOT OF DINNER

The most expensive meal per head was enjoyed by six diners at Petrus in London in July 2001. The bill came to £44,007, which didn't include the cost of the meal itself, which the management happily wiped from the bill. The five-figure total was for the drinks alone, which were as follows: a bottle of Chateau Petrus vintage claret at £12,300; a bottle of Chateau Petrus 1945 at £11,600; a bottle of Chateau Petrus 1946 at £9,400; a bottle of Chateau d'Yquem dessert wine at £9,200; and a bottle of Montrachet 1982 at £1,400. The remaining few pounds and pennies paid for water, cigarettes, fruit juice and champagne.

QUOTE UNQUOTE

How can you govern a country which has 246 varieties of cheese?
CHARLES DE GAULLE, French politician

STRANGE DIETS

Hira Ratan Manek, a retired engineer from Calicut in Kerala, claims to be able to live without solid food. He regularly embarks on long fasts, and says he has conquered hunger by absorbing solar energy through his eyes. He believes people can induce changes in their bodies by gazing at the sun every day during the first hour of sunrise or last hour of sunset while standing barefoot on the ground.

He said: 'After a few days of practice, you will feel the energy entering the body through the eyes. By receiving the sun rays through the eyes, the brain gets charged and brings out its unutilised powers.'

On 1 January 2000, Manek, who was then 65 years old, began his longest fast to date, which lasted 411 days. He drank boiled water between 11am and 4pm but consumed no other liquids or solids. He was kept under strict observation by an array of doctors and specialists, who reported that he remained in surprisingly good health. He lost 19kg in weight, but the weight loss did stabilise. The supervising doctors reported that his pulse and respiration rate slowed, but his brain function and mental capacity were unaffected.

Mr Manek said: 'Solar energy absorbed through the eyes eliminates mental illness, physical illness, spiritual ignorance and makes life happy and peaceful. One's hunger just disappears. It also activates the dormant human brain and awakens the infinite powers in human beings.'

SWEENEY TODD

Sweeney Todd was an apocryphal serial killer, a barber who used his barbershop as a way of finding victims. He fashioned a trapdoor under his barber's chair to quickly dispose of the bodies into the cellar. He had been killing for quite a while before he met the widow Mrs Lovett who became his lover and he began to supply her with meat for her pies. The barber's cellar was linked to the cellar and bakery of the pie shop through the catacombs of St Dunstan's Church where Sweeney Todd would dispose of any parts of the body not suitable for pies. The pair were discovered when churchgoers complained of a putrid smell and the bodies and the subterranean route between pie shop and barber shop was discovered.

Mrs Lovett, after admitting the whole story, escaped the hangman by taking poison in prison. Sweeney Todd was on trial for just one murder, as, despite the bodies being found, it was almost impossible to prove his involvement in their deaths in the age before forensic evidence. However, a conviction for one murder would be enough to send Todd to the gallows.

The story – an amalgam of fact, fiction and bloodthirsty exaggeration – was retold in penny novels, stage plays, films and finally in a musical written by Stephen Sondheim, subtitled the *Demon Barber of Fleet Street*.

Sweeney Todd has since become a popular name for barbers and hairdressers everywhere – and for a pie shop in Reading.

THE DELIA EFFECT

In the 1970s, TV chef Delia Smith recommended a particular type of lemon zester on her show, which not only boosted the sales of that implement but also added a new phrase to the English lexicon: 'doing a Delia'. In 1995, Delia used cranberries in a recipe and sales leapt by 200%. In 1998, she demonstrated, to the derision of her fellow chefs, how to cook an egg. In the six weeks that followed, sales of fresh eggs rose by 58 million. When she also recommended her favourite omelette pan, sales leapt from 200 a year to 90,000 in four months. Sales of prunes, Maldon Crystal Salt Flakes, sunblush tomatoes and skewers (for testing cakes) rocketed after a mention on the show. But in 2003 she received the ultimate accolade: the *Collins English Dictionary* listed 'a Delia dish' among its entries, which preserved for ever her place in our culinary culture.

LITERARY FEASTS

Tamora: Why hast thou slain thine only daughter thus?

Titus Andronicus: Not I; 'twas Chiron and Demetrius:
They ravish'd her, and cut away her tongue;
And they, 'twas they, that did her all this wrong.

Saturninus: Go fetch them hither to us presently.

Titus Andronicus: Why, there they are both, baked in that pie;
Whereof their mother daintily hath fed,
Eating the flesh that she herself hath bred.
'Tis true, 'tis true; witness my knife's sharp point.
                                            Kills Tamora

**William Shakespeare rounds off the blood-letting in *Titus Andronicus*
with a satisfying blend of murder, betrayal and cannibalism.**

FOOD FOR THOUGHT

Ten things that are banned in organic food

Aspartame – artificial sweetener that can cause dizziness, nausea, headaches and diarrhoea

Genetic modification – can cause allergic reactions

Herbicides – destroy the life of the soil and reduce plant and wildlife species

Hydrogenated fat – linked to heart disease

Monosodium glutamate – can cause dizziness, headaches and asthma attacks

Phosphoric acid – linked to osteoporosis

Sulphur dioxide – can cause problems for asthmatics

Hormones – the level of artificial hormones in food and water can upset our individual hormone levels

Artificial colourings – have been linked to allergies and hyperactivity in children

Artificial flavourings – why would you need them?

QUOTE UNQUOTE

*I was polishing off the last mouthful of a dish in a restaurant when
I heard one waiter whisper to another, 'He's actually eating it.'*
GILBERT HARDING, television presenter

RECORD BREAKERS

Simon Sang Koon Sung (Singapore) made 8,192 noodle strings from a single piece of dough in 59.29 seconds at a rate of over 138 per second. The record was set at the Singapore Food Festival on 31 July 1994.

LOST IN TRANSLATION

The following linguistic disasters have been found on menus all over the world, as chefs attempt to translate their culinary delights into English:

Beef rashers beaten up in the country peoples fashion – Poland
Boiled frogfish – Europe
Buttered saucepans and fried hormones – Japan
Cock in wine/Lioness cutlet – Cairo
Cold shredded children and sea blubber in spicy sauce – China
Dreaded veal cutlet with potatoes in cream – China
French creeps – LA
French fried ships – Cairo
Fried fishermen — Japan
Fried friendship – Nepal
Garlic coffee – Europe
Goose barnacles – Spain
Indonesian Nazi goreng – Hong Kong
Muscles of marines/lobster thermos – Cairo
Pork with fresh garbage – Vietnam
Prawn cock and tail – Cairo
Rainbow trout, fillet streak, popotoes, chocolate mouse – Hong Kong
Roasted duck let loose – Poland
Sole bonne femme (Fish landlady style) – Europe
Strawberry crap – Japan
Sweat from the trolley – Europe
Teppan yaki, before your cooked right eyes – Japan
Toes with butter and jam – Bali

COOKING CONUNDRUMS

I can sizzle like bacon,
I am made with an egg,
I have plenty of backbone, but lack a good leg,
I peel layers like onions, but still remain whole,
I can be long, like a flagpole, yet fit in a hole,
What am I?
Answer on page 153

As his fiancée's Sweetbread Special crawled through his digestive system, Frobisher wondered if it was too late to call off the wedding.

LITERARY FEASTS

In the restaurant on Rue Saint-Augustin, M. Mirande [Yves Mirande, a French author and gourmand] would dazzle his juniors, French and American, by dispatching a lunch of raw Bayonne ham and fresh figs, a hot sausage in crust, spindles of filleted pike in a rich rose sauce Nantua, a leg of lamb larded with anchovies, artichokes on a pedestal of foie gras, and four or five kinds of cheese, with a good bottle of Bordeaux and one of champagne, after which he would call for the Armagnac and remind Madame to have ready for dinner the larks and ortolans she had promised him, with a few langoustes and a turbot – and, of course, a fine civet made from the marcassin, or young wild boar, that the lover of the leading lady in his current production had sent up from his estate in the Sologne. 'And while I think of it,' I once heard him say, 'we haven't had any woodcock for days, or truffles baked in the ashes, and the cellar is becoming a disgrace – no more '34s and hardly any '37s. Last week, I had to offer my publisher a bottle that was far too good for him, simply because there was nothing between the insulting and the superlative.'

AJ Liebling, *Between Meals: An Appetite for Paris*

LUCKY FOOD

A few British superstitions

Hot cross buns
The cross in a hot cross bun signifies the Crucifixion. As this took place on Good Friday, it is considered lucky to eat at least one of these buns on Good Friday. Also, it is said that if you hang one in your home, the building will be protected from bad luck or fire.

Blackberries
It is considered unlucky to pick blackberries after 29 September as the Devil is supposedly in them. However, this is probably because the blackberrying season is mostly over by then, and the only remaining blackberries would not be at their best.

Nuts
If you put two nuts into the fire side by side, and give them names – yours and your true love's – it is a good sign if they glow and burn together, but if one or both burst, it means bad luck. A couple can also place two nuts in the fire to see if they will have a long and happy life together.

Apples
When bobbing for apples, the bigger the apple you seize, the greater fortune it will bring you.

Parsley
In folklore, parsley is a highly dangerous plant; one should never plant it, only allow it to seed itself. One old wives' tale even suggests that only the wicked can grow it. It is unlucky to give parsley or transplant it, as transplanting it foretells a death in the family. And if you eat parsley when pregnant, it was said to cause a miscarriage, or prevent conception in the first place. But other superstitions suggest that if a young woman sows parsley-seed she will have a child.

Baby food
Scottish folklore says that a newborn baby should swallow fresh butter to protect against fairies (although don't try this at home). Alternatively, if the child is presented with a new-laid egg, piece of bread and a pinch of salt, it will always have the essentials of life.

SQUARE MEAL

British war ships in the 1700s did not have the best of living conditions, and when ships were away from shore for long periods of time, meals suffered. A sailor's breakfast and lunch were sparse meals consisting of little more than bread and a beverage. But the third meal of the day included meat and was served on a square tray (eating a substantial meal onboard a ship required a tray to carry it all). Hence a 'square meal' was the most substantial meal served.

The eyes of a roasted lamb's head are considered to be delicacies offered to honoured guests in Saudi Arabia.

In most countries of the Middle East, lamb's or calf's brains are commonly sold by butchers and sought after by many a housewife.

Camel humps, feet and meat have been eaten for centuries by people in Chinese and Arab cultures. The extremely tough and sour-tasting hump is first marinated and then roasted. Feet are boiled with herbs and served with a vinaigrette dressing.

Cock's combs (*crette de coq*) are often used by French and Italian chefs to garnish various poultry dishes. Gourmets claim that cock's combs are very tasty, if a little chewy.

In Central and South America iguana meat is sautéed, then casseroled, a dish considered to be a gastronomic delight.

Eskimos consider seal blubber and whale fat to be very tasty. Cod tongues and seal flipper pie are Newfoundland specialities, and regularly found on restaurant menus.

Australian aboriginals consider chopped marinated kangaroo tail ragout to be delicious.

Rooke pie was an old English pub speciality but is almost never served these days.

For centuries, both bear paw and steak have been highly prized in China, Russia and eastern European countries. Today it is almost impossible to buy bear meat commercially, but hunters still can find recipes in old eastern European cook books.

Shark fins and birds' nests, especially those from southern Java, Indonesia, are considered to be delicacies by Chinese gourmets, particularly in Hong Kong. Both are available dried in Hong Kong, Singapore and North America, and used for delicious soups.

Live snake meat is readily available in Singapore, Hong Kong and Taiwan. Sautéed snake meat and snake soup are said to ward off common colds, and to be a healthy dish.

In both Spain and Mexico, the testicles of steers killed in bullfights are considered to be delicacies, and are served grilled with butter and olive oil-based sauces.

QUOTE UNQUOTE

There is no such thing as a little garlic.
AGA KHAN III, former Islamic leader

A TASTY READ

Babycakes, Armistead Maupin
The Ballad of the Sad Café, Carson McCullers
Breakfast at Tiffany's, Truman Capote
Cakes and Ale, Somerset Maugham
Christmas Pudding, Nancy Mitford
Cider with Rosie, Laurie Lee
The Cider House Rules, John Irving
A Clockwork Orange, Anthony Burgess
Dinner at the Homesick Restaurant, Anne Tyler
Eating People is Wrong, Malcolm Bradbury
The Edible Woman, Margaret Atwood
Eggs, Beans and Crumpets, PG Wodehouse
The Famished Road, Ben Okri
The Grapes of Wrath, John Steinbeck
The Ginger Man, JP Donleavy
An Ice-Cream War, William Boyd
Lamb, Bernard McLaverty
The Naked Lunch, William Burroughs
Oranges Are Not The Only Fruit, Jeanette Winterson
The Pumpkin Eater, Penelope Mortimer
Sacred Hunger, Barry Unsworth
Sour Sweet, Timothy Mo
The Sugar House, Antonia White
Whisky Galore, Compton Mackenzie
Who Was Oswald Fish? AN Wilson

STRANGE DIETS

An Indian woman has become famous for her habit of eating huge chunks of ice every day for the last 15 years. Shanti Devi from Bhiwani in Haryana eats up to 3kg of ice every day in cold weather and up to 10kg in the summer. She started eating ice when she was advised it would relieve her severe stomach ache and has never stopped.

The woman, known locally as the 'Ice Grandma', says she cannot sleep without eating ice but has been advised by her doctor to reduce her intake because of old age. The 81-year-old told *United News of India* in 2003: 'I am taking ice daily for the last 15 years in all seasons. During hot days I consume between 8-10kgs but these days due to doctor's restriction I eat only 2-3kgs ice.'

Shanti Devi's son Badlu Ram pointed out that he found it difficult initially to arrange large quantities of ice for his mother, but neighbours had helped out by offering ice stocked in their refrigerators.

The reason many people cry when chopping onions is that slicing an onion breaks down the cell walls, which release enzymes. These break down other substances released from the same cells, some of which – amino acid sulphoxides, to be precise – form a volatile gas. When this reaches your eyes, it irritates the nerve endings, so your brain tells the tear ducts to produce water to dilute the irritation. The trick to reduce the gases is to prevent them from reaching your eyes. There are many theories about how best to prevent onion tears, but some are better than others...

Solution: Wear goggles.
Effectiveness: High, although you'll look silly.

Solution: Cut the onion under water or under a running tap as you slice.
Effectiveness: High, and your hands don't smell as much.

Solution: Light a candle near where you're chopping; the flame burns up some of the noxious fumes and wafts away the rest.
Effectiveness: Intriguingly, this works pretty well.

Solution: Peel onion and place in refrigerator before slicing.
Effectiveness: Moderate to high – the change in temperature alters the compounds in the onion, so reduces the amount of gas.

Solution: Use a food processor. Fling chopped onion into saucepan, slam on lid, then retreat 10 paces until any excess gas has dispersed.

Effectiveness: Moderate to high. As the onion is chopped in an enclosed bowl, the gas is contained.

Solution: Cook onion before you slice it.
Effectiveness: Moderate to high, as change in temperature affects the compounds (see refrigerator theory, left). However, messy and somewhat impractical.

Solution: Hold a lemon, piece of bread, piece of chocolate, sugar cube etc in your mouth, which will help to absorb excess gas.
Effectiveness: Low. The chocolate suggestion is clearly just an excuse.

Solution: Breathe through your mouth while slicing. The theory is that you suck the gas in before it reaches your eyes, then blow more gas away as you exhale, which should help, but doesn't really.
Effectiveness: Low (and your nose starts to run).

TREMENDOUS TOFFEE

The largest piece of toffee ever made weighed 1,335.5kg (2,940lb) and was made by Susie's South Forty Confections Ltd in the USA in 2001 in the shape of the state of Texas. It contained a total of 7,056,000 calories.

REALLY USEFUL RESEARCH

Researchers at the University of Illinois conducted a survey in 2003 to find what kind of food men and women choose to cheer themselves up. The results showed that, apart from ice cream, there is a marked difference between the sexes:

Women	Men
Ice cream	Ice cream
Anything chocolate	Pizza
Biscuits and cakes	Steaks and burgers
Crisps	Pasta
Sweets	Macaroni and cheese, mashed potatoes, green bean casserole

The conclusion that the researchers drew was that men wanted home-cooked food like mother used to make, whereas women wanted instant food that they didn't have to prepare.

CHEESE ROLLING

Every year in Gloucestershire, an 8lb Double Gloucester cheese is rolled down the steep hill at Cooper's Hill, followed at breakneck speed by up to 20 competitors hurling themselves down the hill in its wake. The first person to arrive at the foot of the hill wins the cheese, and this is a sufficient reward for competitors to risk the extremely steep and uneven slope. Minor injuries are virtually guaranteed, and yet competitors (particularly the successful ones) enter the race year after year.

It is not known exactly when the annual Gloucestershire 'Cheese Rolling and Wake' began, but there is evidence that it was already an established tradition in the early 1800s. It could have evolved from ancient fertility rites, hopes of a successful harvest or to safeguard the 'Commoners' Rights' of the inhabitants of the hill.

During the rationing period of 1941–1954 a wooden substitute was used, which had a small niche that contained a token piece of cheese. When, as occasionally happens, the race has to be cancelled, a small ceremony takes place with a single cheese rolled, to maintain the tradition.

Geoffrey Willans and Ronald Searle gave new meaning to the term *enfant terrible* when they created their fictional schools of St Trinian's and St Custard's. As any fule kno, Nigel Molesworth was their most memorable pupil who kept an enlightening if very badly spelled diary of his school days. His diaries appear in four volumes, of which *Down with Skool*, from which this extract is taken, is the first:

On Etiqutte:

Many boys find themselves quite incapable of making any rude comments on skool food. This is hardly good maners hem-hem and i must impress on all cads and bounders who sa poo gosh when they see a skool sossage to mend their ways.

When faced with a friteful piece of meat which even the skool dog would refuse do not screw up the face in any circs and sa coo ur gosh ghastly. This calls attention to oneself and makes it more difficult to pinch a beter piece from the next boy.

Rice PUDINGS and jely in the poket are not a good mixture with fluff and the ushual nauseating contents. Sometimes you can chiz a bit of pink mange into a hankchief but it is apt to be a bit hard to manage when bloing the nose. peason hav tried green peas up the sleeve but no good really as they all come shooting down again.

On Being at Table:

Acktually whatever boys may sa about skool food the moment deaf master sa lord make us truly etc. whole skool descend upon food with roar like an H bomb and in 2 minits all have been swept bare. We then hav time for interval of uplifting conversation.

i sa e.g. i think aldous huxley is rather off form in point counterpoint, peason. And he repli i simply couldn't agree with you more rat face but

peason is very 4th rate and hav not got beyond buldog drummond. Anyway then the next course come and all boys disappear in a cloud of jely blanch mange plums and aple while treacle tart fly in all directions.

On Withdrawal:

When the repast is finished the head of the skool or headmaster should wait for a moment until the conversation shows some small signs of flagging then rising to his feet he indicates that the meal is at an end and the lades may withdraw.

Acktually if he waited for the conversation to flag he would be sitting there until tea time when it would all begin agane. Wot he does is to bawl Silence at the top of his voice separate three tuoughs who are fiting and the whole skool charge into the corridor except molesworth 2 who is pinching the radio malt.

OLD PICTURE, NEW CAPTION

It was fortunate for Wilson that, after his little accident, Cook's mulligatawny soup was found to be remarkably effective as a gentleman's hair restorer.

THE DEVIL'S PORRIDGE

In 1915, Britain seemed in danger of losing the war through lack of munitions, until 30,000 men and women turned up for work at a factory on the Solway in a quiet corner of rural Scotland to help mix the 'Devil's Porridge'. This was a highly explosive mixture of nitro-glycerine and nitro-cotton, which was so volatile that the factory workers who 'kneaded' the porridge could not wear any loose items of jewellery or clothing in case they fell into the mixture. The paste was dried, rolled into lengths called cordite and put into shells and bullets. The sheer number of workers involved meant that the factory could turn out 1,000 tonnes of the paste every week, more than all the other plants in Britain put together. The factory had its own railway with 125 miles of track, its own power station and water treatment centre and its own bakery to feed the workers, and two new towns were built to house them. The poetic name of Devil's Porridge was coined by Sir Arthur Conan Doyle, after he visited the factory in 1918.

EIGHT FOODS OF LOVE

Agape – a frugal meal that early Christians took together: from the Greek *agape*, meaning 'love'

Amourettes – spinal bone marrow of beef, veal or mutton

Baiser – a French *petit four* of two meringues joined with cream or buttercream

Hearts of palm – the buds of certain palm trees that can be eaten raw in a salad

Lovage – an aromatic herb with a taste similar to celery

Kissing crust – the pale, slightly underbaked part of the crust left where one loaf touched another

Kissel – a Russian dessert made of sweetened and thickened red fruit purée

Liaison – any mixture or ingredient used to bind or thicken sauces, soups or stews

Puits d'amour – a small pastry made of two rounds of puff pastry sandwiched together with jam or confectioner's custard

WHO WAS FANNY ADAMS?

The origin of the phrase 'sweet Fanny Adams' – abbreviated to 'sweet FA', with unfortunate connotations – has a gruesome origin. Fanny Adams was a child who in 1867 was horribly murdered and dismembered. The Royal Navy, perhaps unmoved by her fate, began to use her name to refer to their ration of tinned mutton, which was introduced about the same time. It then meant 'something worthless', and now means 'nothing at all'.

FABULOUS FLAPJACK

A piece of flapjack was invented in 2003 that could revolutionise the diagnosis of several fatal diseases. The supersnack was devised by researchers at the University of Dundee with the help of Alan Clark, the owner of a family-run bakery in the city. Each flapjack contains a small amount of tracer – the naturally occurring stable isotope of carbon – which can be detected by a breath test after it has been eaten. Doctors can then detect whether and how quickly the cake has been absorbed into the patient's system, which can indicate whether a patient is suffering from a bowel disorder, which impairs the digestion of medication used to treat diabetes, irritable bowel syndrome and Aids. The new flapjack method could become a widespread alternative to using radioactive tracers, and would be much tastier.

COOKS IN BOOKS

When I cooked on a charter yacht in the United States, I wanted to bring back some steamer clams and Maine lobster for my brother, to convince him that New England seafood was the best. The customs officer heard the lobsters scrabbling away in my bag and said I couldn't bring them through if they were alive. Can I if they are dead? I asked. Yes, said the customs officer. So I took off my brooch in order to drive the pin through the brain of each lobster. What are you doing? said the officer. I was planning to kill them, I replied. Not in front of me, you're not, says the officer. So I got them through alive.

Clarissa Dickson-Wright, *Cooking with the Two Fat Ladies*

TAKE ONE TRUFFLE TWICE DAILY

When chocolate was first brought to Europe, physicians used it as a medicine, as it was considered to be an effective treatment for a wide range of illnesses. These included:

anaemia
consumption
emaciation
faintness of heart
gout
kidney stones
low virility
mental fatigue
physical fatigue
poor appetite
poor bowel function
poor breast milk production
poor digestion
poor kidney function
shortness of breath
sluggish nervous system
tuberculosis

QUOTE UNQUOTE

The most remarkable thing about my mother is that for 30 years she served the family nothing but leftovers. The original meal has never been found.
SAM LEVINSON, US comic

EXPERT ADVICE

How to tell when your roast is done

Insert a metal skewer into the thickest part of the joint. Leave the skewer in place for 10 seconds, then draw it out and place it on the inside of your wrist.

• If the skewer is cool or barely warm, the meat is uncooked.

• If the skewer is very warm but bearable on your skin, the meat is cooked rare.

• If the skewer is too hot to rest on your skin for more than a second, the meat is well done.

Alternatively, you can just use a meat thermometer: 60°C for medium pink, 80°C for well-done.

THE FOOD OLYMPICS

British Olympic Gold Medal winners with foodie names:

Applegarth, Willie..Athletics (1912)
Bacon, Stanley ....Wrestling (1908)
Berry, Arthur ....Football (1908)
Butler, Guy...Athletics (1920)
Cook, Stephanie ....Modern Pentathlon (2000)
Cooke, Harold ....Hockey (1920)
Cornet, George ....Swimming (1908)
Currie, Lorne..Yachting (1900)
Miller, Charles..Polo (1908)
Miller, George ....Polo (1908)
Pike, JF ....Shooting (1908)

KING ALFRED'S CAKES

So did Alfred the Great really burn any cakes? The much-repeated story is that while retreating from a Viking attack, the King of Wessex took refuge in the swamps of Athelney (a small area in Somerset). There he was given shelter by a peasant woman who, not knowing who he was, asked him to keep an eye on some cakes. His mind no doubt on other things, he allowed the cakes to burn and was ticked off by the aggrieved cook. However, historians agree that this is most likely apocryphal. In reality, Alfred did flee from battle into the Somerset swamps in 878, but swiftly raised an army that defeated a Danish force on the borders of Wiltshire and Somerset and earned England a temporary respite from Viking invasions.

King Alfred's Cakes is also the name for a kind of fungi that grows on dead trees and looks like burnt cakes.

YOU ARE WHAT YOU EAT

The connection between diet and health has been made from the earliest times, most memorably by a Greek physician called Galen, who developed his theories about diet and health in the 1st century AD. The basic theory was that human beings were made up of four 'humours' – blood, bile, phlegm and black bile – which corresponded to the four elements in nature and therefore in food – air, fire, water and earth. So if, for example, a man appeared to have an excess of bile, he would be advised to avoid hot (fire) foods and eat cool (earth) foods instead.

A similar system is still adhered to in China and other Asian countries, where foods are divided into yin (cool) and yang (hot). The only problem in the earliest days of this theory was that there was no basis for deciding which food corresponded to which humour, and the eventual list of foods and humours was somewhat arbitrary.

Galen's medical writings survived translation into Syriac (by the Syrians), then into Arabic (when Syria fell to the Arabs), and finally into Latin by Constantine the African, a learned traveller who settled in Salerno in Italy, where a medical school had grown up after the fall of the Roman empire. By this time, Galen's works had acquired Arabic, Persian, Chinese and Indian influences and new information, all of which formed the basis of medical knowledge for almost 1,500 years.

GUESS WHO'S COMING TO DINNER?

One of the largest banquets ever served took place in the Tuileries Gardens in Paris on 22 November 1900. Emile Loubet, then President of the Republic, invited 22,295 mayors from across France to a Mayors' Banquet, with the intention of reviving their republican spirit. Tents were specially erected in the gardens for the occasion, and the visiting dignitaries were served a feast of Rouen duck loaf, fillet of beef Bellevue, chicken from Bresse and ballotine of pheasant. The waiters covered the four miles of tables on bicycles.

QUOTE UNQUOTE

A cucumber should be well sliced and dressed with pepper and vinegar, and then thrown out as good for nothing.
SAMUEL JOHNSON, writer and diarist

CULINARY LEGENDS

Isabella Beeton (1836-1865) is fondly thought of as a wise and grandmotherly figure, but was in fact only 25 when she published *The Book of Household Management* in 1861. She did not claim to be a trained cook, but compiled recipes and advice from many sources. In the preface she states: 'What moved me in the first instance to attempt a work like this was the discomfort and suffering which I had seen brought upon men and women by household mismanagement. I have always thought that there is no more fruitful source of family discontent than a housewife's badly cooked dinners and untidy ways.'

Having grown up in a household of 21 children, including step-siblings, this view is not surprising. Her book was not just a cookbook but a complete manual to running a home, including chapters on managing servants, basic medical advice and legal matters, running to over 1,000 pages. She had been well educated, and the text is peppered with literary references and discussions on religion, science and history as well as household matters. She no doubt benefited from having a husband who not only was a wealthy publisher but also believed that an intelligent wife was a great blessing in life. Her progressive outlook is reflected in the legal chapter, which details the rights of women separated from their husbands because of ill-treatment. Mrs Beeton's life was productive but tragically brief; she died at the age of 28, of puerperal fever.

SAY IT WITH FOOD

Five porridge proverbs:

He has supped all his porridge – he has eaten his
last meal/he is dead

Keep your breath to cool your porridge – keep your
opinions to yourself

Not to earn salt for one's porridge – to be a layabout

To do porridge – to do time in jail

Everything tastes of porridge – whatever our fantasies may be, the
mundane facts of life remain

COOKING CONUNDRUMS

There are 10 volumes of cookbooks on a kitchen shelf. Each book is two inches thick. The books are lined up in order. A bookworm starts to eat its way through the books, starting with the front cover of Volume One, and finishing with the back cover of Volume 10. He eats in a straight line, so how far does he travel?

Answer on page 153

There are countless festivals of food and drink around the world every year. The following stand out for their deliciousness or absurdity:

Citrus Festival, Menton, France
The lemon capital of France celebrates the end of its **February** harvest with plenty of food and drink and a parade of floats made of huge citrus fruits.

Wildfoods Festival, Hokitika, New Zealand
Brave gourmets descend on New Zealand in **March** to try the latest bush tucker: crickets, slugs, sheep's eyeballs and bull's penis sausage.

Black Pudding Fair, Mortagne au Perche, France
Over three days in **March**, hundreds of exhibitors and butchers keep carnivores and trainee vampires happy with around three miles of black puddings of every size, shape and flavour.

Spamarama, Austin, USA
Originally a sideshow to an **April** Fool's Day gig, the spam stall eventually took centre stage and the whole festival has become, in its own words, 'The Perpetual Pandemonious Party of Pork'.

Bruschetta Festival, Predappio Alta, Italy
The town's inhabitants converge on the square in **May** to witness the making of the world's largest bruschetta. It gets bigger every year, and takes around 95kg of bread, 11kg tomatoes, 10 litres of olive oil and 270 cloves of garlic to make.

Frog Festival, Asciano, Italy
The frogs are invited, but sadly they won't know why till it's too late. This **June** festival is dedicated to this gastronomic delicacy, and includes music, dancing and a frog-filled feast.

Giant Omelette Festival, Granby, Québec
You can't make a giant omelette without breaking 5,000 eggs, which is what five French-speaking cities do every **June** in Québec. Citizens from Abbeville, Bessières and Fréjus in France, Dumbea in New Caledonia and Québec in Canada join forces to create this culinary monster, then share it with the spectators, after a ceremony to 'knight' the omelette chefs. As well as the eggs, the omelette requires 50lbs onions, 52lbs butter, 6.5 gallons milk and 1.5 gallons of cooking oil.

Bull's Testicle Festival, Charlo, Montana, USA
Montana is so fond of its favourite delicacy that it holds more than one of these festivals every year, but the **June** event is the biggest. To go with the macho theme and the food, the celebrations include drinking and a rodeo as well as a parade and plenty of music.

Garlic Festival, Vessalico, Italy
Vessalico grows a particularly savoury form of mountain garlic, and the **July** garlic festival (*Fiera*

dell'Aglio) is a re-enactment of a fair held in 1760, and is rich in history and tradition, including folklore performances, art made from weaving garlic leaves, and an evening ball.

Raspberry Fair, Concèze, France
Every **July**, this tiny village celebrates its key product, the raspberry. There are plenty of opportunities to taste the fruit in many forms, from coulis and granitas to champagne cocktails. Concèze holds the world record for the largest ever raspberry tart, made in 1997, which measured over 3m across.

Eel Festival, Ahus, Sweden
If you like your food wriggly, this is the place to come in **August**, as you can eat eels all day long. The local fisherman deliver the goods, and after you buy your ticket, you can eat all the eels you like.

Heaviest Gooseberry Fair, Egton Bridge, Yorkshire
The **August** competition to find the heaviest gooseberry began in the 19th century, and still attracts hordes of entrants. Past winners have produced a gooseberry the size of a golf ball.

Salt Festival, Salies-de-Bearn, France
September celebrates the town's central well; the water in which is more salty than seawater, brought great wealth to the town in the Middle Ages, when meat was preserved in salt. Lots of history and food, salted and otherwise.

National Hard Crab Derby and Fair, Maryland, USA
As if eating the crabs weren't entertainment enough, you can watch them being raced too. This **September** festival celebrates the crab harvest, a Maryland speciality, with lots of food, a beauty contest (people, not crabs), boat racing, swimming contests, carnival and fireworks.

Giant Pumpkin Contest, Zurich, Switzerland
Switzerland is not normally known for its pumpkins, but this **October** competition has become very popular. Last year's winner weighed in at 341kg, which would make a tremendous Hallowe'en lantern.

Firewater Festival, Potes, Spain
If you like to set your mouth on fire, the **November** *aguardiente fiesta* is the perfect place. At around 40% alcohol, it is not to be drunk lightly. It is a clear spirit flavoured with ingredients such as honey, cherry and coffee, and is brewed locally (and legally). The festival offers tasting opportunities and an evening dance.

Goose fat, the secret to perfect roast potatoes, is celebrated every **December** in Castelnaudary with a market, a dance and a goose fat competition. Castelnaudary is said to be the capital of cassoulet, a sustaining dish invented when the village was under siege from the English, in which goose fat is a key ingredient. Despite the high fat content, the people of this region enjoy a long and healthy life.

SEVEN SAUSAGE FACTS

- The word sausage is derived from the Latin word *salsus,* which means something salted
- Dick Turpin worked as a butcher
- Sausages are eaten at 71% of all UK barbecues
- Queen Victoria liked sausages but insisted that the meat in them be hand-chopped rather than minced
- Sausages were called bangers during World War II because they exploded when fried, due to the high water content
- Ninety per cent of British households buy sausages and 50% buy them at least once a month
- Sausages are mentioned in Homer's *Odyssey* :
  These goat sausages sizzling here in the fire –
  We packed them with fat and blood to have for supper.
  Now, whoever wins this bout and proves the stronger,
  Let that man step up and take his pick of the lot!

BUT IS IT ART?

In 2003, artist Dave Ball created a sculpture out of 10,500 pink wafer biscuits for an exhibition in west Wales called *The Joy of Kitsch*. His sweet work of art was an attempt to recreate Carl Andre's *Equivalent VIII*, the infamous pile of bricks bought by the Tate Gallery in 1972, which caused outrage among art critics and the general public. The manager of Carmarthen's Oriel Myrddin Gallery, where 24-year-old Ball exhibited his edible masterpiece, said that he didn't think that customers would eat the exhibit, but noted that Ball had left them a few spare biscuits, just in case.

LITERARY FEASTS

'Hold hard a minute, then!' said the Rat. He looped the painter through a ring in his landing stage, climbed up into his hole above, and... reappeared staggering under a fat, wicker luncheon basket.

'Shove that under your feet,' he observed to the Mole, as he passed it down into the boat. Then he untied the painter and took the sculls again.

'What's inside it?' asked the Mole, wriggling with curiosity.

'There's cold chicken inside it,' replied the Rat briefly; 'coldtongue-coldhamcoldbeefpickledgherkinssaladfrenchrollscresssandwidgepottedmeatgingerbeerlemonadesodawater-'

'O stop, stop,' cried the Mole in ecstasies: 'This is too much!'

Kenneth Grahame, *The Wind in the Willows*

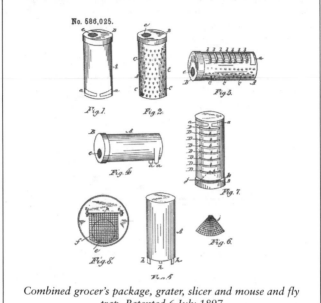

No. 586,025.

Fig.1. *Fig.2.* *Fig.3.*

Fig.4. *Fig.7.*

Fig.6.

Fig.8. *Fig.5.*

Combined grocer's package, grater, slicer and mouse and fly trap. Patented 6 July 1897

FOOD FOR THOUGHT

For every dollar that the World Health Organisation spends on trying to improve the diets of people across the globe, approximately US$500 is spent by the food industry worldwide on promoting processed foods. The food industry spends US$40 billion each year on advertising.

FEAST OF FOOLS

The Feast of Fools was celebration that was thoroughly if rudely enjoyed in the Middle Ages. It was held on the feasts of St Stephen, St John and the Holy Innocents which, conveniently, were on the 26th, 27th and 28th December. Although it centred on a cathedral, the purpose was to mock and disrupt the ceremony, and to indulge in obscene jests and dancing. It was eventually suppressed during the Reformation.

TELL THEM ABOUT THE HONEY

Bees could be among the most important contributors to a healthy diet. Honey, royal jelly, propolis and bee pollen are all thought to have beneficial effects, and bees and their products have been celebrated for tens of thousands of years. And when you learn what is in them, it is not surprising.

Honey is rich in vitamins B, C and calcium. It is a natural form of sugar, which has been proven to improve athletic performance, to help reduce insomnia and to speed the healing of wounds. Studies in New Zealand found that manuka honey taken for a month could eliminate *Helicobacter pylori* from the stomach, a major cause of stomach ulcers, and did so more efficiently than conventional drugs. It is also thought that if hay fever sufferers eat locally produced honey, it helps build their resistance to allergies caused by local pollen. Russian hospitals use honey to help heal burns, and honey has been used to heal varicose leg ulcers. Finally, studies in the UK are finding that honey has powerful anti-bacterial properties and may help in the fight against MRSA, the often fatal infection that plagues our hospitals.

Royal jelly is the food of the Queen bee, secreted by nurse bees to give the queen a lifespan of up to three years (worker bees live about six weeks). It is rich in vitamin B, enzymes, hormones and amino acids. The National Institute of Medical Herbalists say that it is well-known for its anti-viral properties.

Bee pollen is rich in most B vitamins and folic acid and is believed by some to help promote fertility and conception.

Propolis – from a Greek word meaning 'defender of the city' – contains every vitamin except K and every mineral we need apart from sulphur. It is a resinous substance collected by bees from plant buds, which they mix with saliva and use to repair the hive. Russian hospitals prescribe it to aid recovery after surgery.

Needless to say, the purer and fresher the honey, the better, so find a local supplier, rather than a cheap mass-produced blend.

RECORD BREAKERS

The largest pancake in the world was cooked up by the Co-operative Union Ltd in Rochdale in the UK in August 1994. The cooks whipped up a 15.01m pancake, 2.5cm deep, weighing three tonnes.

WHAT'S FOR PUDDING?

Black pudding is a delicacy all over Europe, and like many gourmet delicacies, it has countless regional and national variations. Here are a few things that are added to the key ingredient of pig's blood:

Alsace, France – pork rind and fat, ears, head, trotters and onions
Auvergne, France – milk and crackling; chestnuts
Brittany, France – prunes
Brussels, Belgium – eggs, butter and cream
Flanders – raisins
Lyon, France – raw onions marinated in brandy and herbs
Nancy, France – milk
Normandy, France – apples
Paris, France – cooked onions
Poitou, France – cooked spinach, cream, semolina and eggs
Kerry, Ireland – sheep's blood
Lecce, Italy – pig's brains
Scandinavia – raisins
Sicily – raisins, almonds, candied pumpkin
Spain – onions, rice and flavourings such as aniseed, cloves and other spices, rice, pine nuts

QUOTE UNQUOTE

Cauliflower is nothing but cabbage with a college education.
MARK TWAIN, US novelist

IT'S THE REAL THING

Curry is a much misunderstood food. The original word, *kari,* means simply 'sauce', and refers to a sauce that was poured over rice, lentils or any other food to give it a flavour. However, it was only a relish rather than the bulk of the dish. Also, it was not mouth-burningly hot. Chillis, now an integral part of the very hot curries some people inflict on themselves in a quest for 'authenticity', did not appear in India until the 1500s, when they were introduced there from the Americas. During the era of the East India Company, the Europeans – in an act that may have been a warm-up for the regulatory obsessions of the EEC – devised formulae for the spice mixtures, and in 1889, at the Universal Paris Exhibition, the composition of curry powder was fixed at 34g tamarind, 44g onion, 20g coriander, 5g chilli pepper, 3g turmeric, 2g cumin, 3g fenugreek, 2g pepper and 2g mustard. However, in India, the spices vary almost infinitely according to the region, caste, customs and the whims and preferences of the cook.

FOOD FOR THOUGHT

A 2003 study by mineralogist David Thomas concluded that nutrient levels in the UK's fruit and vegetables have fallen significantly in the last 50 years. His report found that, on average, vegetables had lost 16% of their potassium content, 24% of magnesium, 27% of iron, 46% of calcium, 49% of sodium and 76% of copper. For fruit, the average losses were 15% of magnesium, 16% of calcium, 19% of copper, 22% of potassium, 24% of iron and 29% of sodium. In the same period, the sugar content of some fruits had risen, and had almost doubled from 8% to 15% in certain types of apple. Another researcher, Anne-Marie Mayer at Cornell University, carried out a similar study and had almost identical findings. Both researchers connect the decline in nutrients to the modernising of farming techniques that occurred over the same period. However, the Food Standards Authority in the UK has warned against drawing such conclusions and is launching its own nutrient study.

COOKING CONUNDRUMS

You have three boxes of fruit. One contains just apples, one contains just oranges, and one contains a mixture of both. Each box is labelled – one says 'apples', one says 'oranges', and one says 'apples and oranges'. However, it is known that none of the boxes are labelled correctly. How can you label the boxes correctly if you are only allowed to take a look at just one piece of fruit from just one of the boxes?

Answer on page 153

I WOULDN'T EAT THAT IF I WERE YOU

The viscera of Japanese *abalone* (sea snails) can harbour a poisonous substance, which causes a burning, stinging, prickling and itching over the entire body. The symptoms do not arise until the sufferer is exposed to sunlight, but if the sea snails are actually eaten outdoors in sunlight, the symptoms occur immediately and may even cause skin lesions. It is believed the toxin may come from seaweed ingested by the abalone. Nevertheless, sea snails are a delicacy in Japan and China.

Mexican food is delicious and perfectly safe as long as you are careful never to get any of it in your digestive system.
DAVE BARRY, writer and columnist

WEBSITES FOR OBSESSIVES

www.carrotmuseum.com
The home of the World Carrot Museum, a virtual institution that will tell you everything you need to know about this humble vegetable.
www.cheese.com
Although this is a sales site, it does list every cheese you will ever want to eat or identify.
www.cheeseracing.com
What happens when you put processed cheese on a barbecue.
www.chocolate.org
Less about eating and more about science, this links to lots of academic research about chocolate. If you eat a lot of chocolate, this can help you to justify your habit.
www.chocophile.com
Full of mouthwatering articles and news, and updated regularly, with links to lots of good chocolatiers.
www.foodsubs.com
Identifies every ingredient you can think of, so particularly useful for exotic produce and for deciphering UK/US terms.
www.nicecupoftea andasitdown.com
Cheerfully daft and very extensive; offers more information on biscuits than you'll need, including answers to such questions as 'Is a Jaffa cake a biscuit?' and 'What's the story with pink wafers?' Log on for biscuit of the week, a survey of fig rolls and how to make underpant toast.
www.sausagelinks.com
Sausage information, sausage of the week and sausage news.
www.soupsong.com
Utterly wonderful, seemingly endless and the best source of soup jokes in the universe, such as US comic Steven Wright's immortal line: 'I put instant soup in the microwave and almost went back in time.'
www.tea.co.uk
Interesting and varied site run by the Tea Council, which, though largely grown-up and sensible, is frivolous enough to offer a daily tealeaf reading.

LITERARY FEASTS

Surely everyone is aware of the divine pleasures which attend a wintry fireside; candles at four o'clock, warm hearth-rugs, tea, a fair tea-maker, shutters closed, curtains flowing in ample draperies to the floor, whilst the wind and rain are raging audibly without.
Thomas de Quincey, *Confessions of an English Opium-Eater*

CULINARY LEGENDS

Marcus Gavius Apicius, born about 25 AD, is believed to be the author of one of the world's oldest cookbooks, *De Re Coquinaria Libri Decem* (Cuisine in Ten Books) He was known for his expensive tastes, and was perhaps the original inventor of the idea of foie gras, as he devised a way of feeding dried figs to pigs to fatten their livers. According to the *Larousse Gastronomique*, he spent extravagantly on numerous banquets, and when he ran out of money, he preferred to poison himself rather than scale back his lifestyle.

WHO EATS THE MOST?

Food	Country consuming greatest amount	Position of UK in top 10
Baked beans	Ireland	2nd
Canned food	Sweden	2nd
Chewing gum	Andorra	Not in top 10
Chocolate	Switzerland	4th
Coffee	Finland	Not in top 10
Crisps	UK	1st
Frozen food	Denmark	5th
Ice cream	Australia	Not in top 10
Meat	US	Not in top 10
Soft drinks, fizzy	US	9th
Sugar	Macedonia	Not in top 10
Tea	Ireland	4th

WHO PUT THE HONEY IN HONEYMOON?

The origin of the word honeymoon has several explanations. The OED lists 'honey-month' used in 1564 to refer to the first month after marriage, and 'honeymoon', used in 1696, to denote the same. This is thought to arise from the custom for a newly married couple to drink a potion containing honey every day for the first month of their marriage. A similar explanation is that in Saxon times newlyweds would eat honey every day, as it was thought not only to promote fertility but also to provide the necessary desire and stamina to start a family. A less happy explanation suggests that it refers to the waning of the affection of newlyweds after one month, just as the moon wanes after a month. Current usage backs this up – we tend to refer to the early trouble-free days in any venture (a new business, a new government) as 'the honeymoon period' – when optimism rules and all mistakes are lovingly forgiven before reality sets in.

THEY SAID WHAT?

Catchphrases that are good enough to eat:

It's all done in the best possible taste – Kenny Everett

Beulah, peel me a grape – Mae West in *I'm No Angel*

Dig for victory – wartime slogan from Sir Reginald Dorman Smith

Goody goody yum yum – theme tune lyric of 70s comedy
show *The Goodies*

He can't fart and chew gum at the same time – President Lyndon
Johnson's description of President Gerald Ford

He can't walk and chew gum at the same time – revised comment by
Johnson when Ford was elected in 1974

Here's a pretty kettle of fish – Queen Mary, referring to the
abdication crisis of 1936

If you can't stand the heat, get out of the kitchen – President Harry
Truman, on his decision not to stand for election in 1952

No such thing as a free lunch – 19th century saying immortalised by
Milton Friedman in the title of his book

Pass the sick-bag, Alice – used by John Junor in his
Sunday Express column

Pile it high, sell it cheap – Sir John Cohen, founder of Tesco

Probably the best lager in the world – Carlsberg advertisement,
unforgettably voiced by Orson Welles

The thinking-man's crumpet – coined by Frank Muir to describe
broadcaster Joan Bakewell

QUOTE UNQUOTE

*Wit ought to be a glorious treat, like caviar. Never spread it about
like marmalade.*
NOEL COWARD, actor, dramatist and songwriter

FOOD FOR THOUGHT

Cases of deficiency in respect of pleasures, that is of enjoying them
less than one ought, hardly occur; because such insensibility is sub-
human. Even the lower animals discriminate between different
foods, and enjoy some but not others. If there is any creature to
whom nothing is pleasant and everything indifferent, he must be
very far from being human; and because such a type hardly occurs,
it has not secured itself a name.

Aristotle, *Ethics*

LONDON ROADS OF FOOD

A tasty amble through the streets of London:

Artichoke Hill, SE5 • Bacon Grove, SE1 • Cheddar Close, N11
• Duck Lane, W1 • Eatington Road, E10 • Frying Pan Alley, E1•
Grocer's Hall Court, EC2 • Ham Yard, W1 • Ive Farm Lane, E10
• Juniper Lane, E6 • Kitcat Terrace E3 • Lime Street, EC3 •
Milk Street, EC2 • Nutmeg Lane, E14 • Oat Lane, EC2 •
Pudding Lane, EC3 • Quorn Road, SE22 • Rye Lane, SE15 •
Sugar Bakers Court, EC3 • Tamarind Court, W8 • Upper Ham
Road, Richmond • Vinegar Street E1 • Walnut Gardens E15 •
Yorkshire [because you think of Pudding] Road, E14

LUCKY FOOD

A few American superstitions

Before slicing a new loaf of bread, make the sign of the cross on it.

A loaf of bread should never be turned upside down after a slice has been cut from it.

A fish should always be eaten from the head toward the tail.

To drop a fork means a man is coming to visit.

If you bite your tongue while eating, it is because you have recently told a lie.

An onion cut in half and placed under the bed of a sick person will draw off fever and poisons.

A wish will come true if you make it while burning onions.

If you spill pepper you will have a serious argument with your best friend.

Rosemary planted by the doorstep will keep witches away.

Salty soup is a sign that the cook is in love.

If a single woman sleeps with a piece of wedding cake under her pillow, she will dream of her future husband.

It's bad luck to let milk boil over.

QUOTE UNQUOTE

I no longer prepare food or drink with more than one ingredient.
CYRA MCFADDEN, journalist and novelist

A SHORT ESSAY ON CHRISTMAS PUDDING

What we now know as Christmas pudding was first made as a Christmas Eve dish of frumenty, a soupy dish of hulled wheat cooked in milk. In the early Middle Ages, it was made with meat broth, oatmeal, eggs, currants, dried plums and spices and was known as 'plum porridge', or 'pottage'. It was served with the first course and eaten with a spoon and was a favourite of Henry VIII. In Elizabethan times, it became thicker as they replaced the oats with breadcrumbs and added suet and ale or wine.

Oliver Cromwell banned it in 1664, disapproving of its boozy contents, calling it 'a lewd custom'. But Cromwell failed to abolish either the monarchy or Christmas pudding, and George I reinstated the dish 50 or so years later. By this time we had learned how to steam it in a pudding cloth, and it took on a perfectly round 'cannonball' shape. The Victorians took out the plums and added raisins, currants and dried peel. Finally, in the 20th century it was poured into a basin, covered with the pudding cloth and steamed, thereby taking on its most recent shape.

But the most important thing to know about Christmas pudding is how to set it alight successfully. The secret is to gently warm the brandy in a pan first, scoop some up in an heatproof ladle, set fire to the brandy, and then pour it on to the pudding.

COOKING CONUNDRUMS

What does an anthropophagist eat?
Answer on page 153

CULINARY LEGENDS

Marie Antoine Carême (1783-1833) was the founder and architect of French *haute cuisine*. He was one of at least 25 children born to an impoverished family whose father put him out on the street at the age of about 10 to make his own way in the world. Fortunately, he knocked on the door of a restaurant to ask for a job. By the age of 21, he was chef de cuisine to Talleyrand, Louis XVIII's foreign minister. Carême also served as head chef to the future George IV of England, Emperor Alexander I of Russia, and Baron James de Rothschild. He wrote several voluminous works on cookery, which included hundreds of recipes, menus, history of French cookery, instructions for organising kitchens, and instructions for his signature dishes, monumental architectural constructions of food called *pièces montées*. He died at the age of 50, and is remembered as the 'chef of kings and the king of chefs'.

COOKS IN BOOKS

Nothing could be easier, on the face of it, than this stupid scullion work, but it is astonishingly hard when one is in a hurry. One has to leap to and fro between a multitude of jobs – it is like sorting a pack of cards against the clock. You are, for example, making toast, when bang! down comes a service lift with an order for tea, rolls and three different kinds of jam, and simultaneously bang! down comes another demanding scrambled eggs, coffee and grapefruit; you run to the kitchen for the eggs and to the dining-room for the fruit, going like lightning so as to be back before your toast burns, and having to remember about the tea and coffee, besides half a dozen other orders that are still pending; and at the same time some waiter is following you and making trouble about a lost bottle of soda-water, and you are arguing with him. It needs more brains than you think.

George Orwell, *Down and Out in Paris and London*

SAY IT WITH FOOD

Phrases to leave you hungry…

Adam's ale – water
Banyan day – a meat-free day, as recorded by the English navy; the day when their rations included no meat
'Tis a Barmecide's feast – a disappointing illusion (from the Barmecide family in *Arabian Nights*)
To dine with Democritus (or with Duke Humphrey, or with the cross-legged knights) – to get no dinner
To give one a baker's dozen – to give someone a beating (the baker's dozen representing one blow too many)
I'll give him beans – I'll give him a thrashing
The big gooseberry season – silly season for the newspapers
To eat dog – to perform an unpleasant task for another. American Indians ate dogs at important meetings, a custom to which white men took

exception. They were eventually allowed to offer a silver dollar for someone else to eat the dog for them
To eat one's terms – to be studying for the bar. Students have to eat in the hall of an Inn of Court at least three times in each of the 12 terms before they are called to the bar
To eat the leek – to eat one's words
To take bread and salt – to take an oath
To return to our muttons – to get back to the subject
To pepper one well – to give someone a beating, or shoot at them
To have a finger in every pie – to be involved in or have a share in; not usually meant as a compliment
The old woman is cooking a goose – child's phrase for 'it's snowing'.

WHAT DID YOU COOK IN THE WAR, GRANDMA?

In World War II, ration books appeared in September 1939 and by January 1940 the first items of food were being rationed. Each person was restricted to 4oz bacon or ham and 4oz of butter per week. As the war went on the list of rationed food got longer. At its peak, in August 1942, the allowance for each person per week was:

1s 2d worth of meat (eg a pork chop and four sausages)
8oz of sugar
8oz of butter, margarine or lard
4oz of bacon or ham (eg four rashers of bacon)
2oz of tea (half a packet or the equivalent of 15 teabags)
2oz of cheese
1 egg

Jam, rice, dried fruit, canned tomatoes and peas, breakfast cereals and condensed milk, chocolate, sweets, biscuits and oat flakes were also rationed.

The unexpected result was that everyone ate better because they ate less fat, less meat and more vegetables. Also, because everyone got the same, the poor often ate as well as the rich, and better than they had before the war. Farming increased and imports decreased as people went back to the land. Nearly half the families in London had an allotment or a garden to grow their own vegetables and salads. They even grew cabbages in Kensington Gardens.

DO NOT ADJUST YOUR TOASTER

In 2003, researchers at Leeds University spent three months calculating a scientific formula for the making of perfect toast. They concluded that the solution lay in achieving the correct relationship between the heat of the bread and the temperature and weight of the butter. While the mathematical formula is of no use to most of us at the breakfast table, the researchers did make some useful recommendations, including:

a) that the bread needs to reach 120°C to turn golden brown;
b) that the butter should be taken from the fridge and spread on the toast within two minutes of its popping up from the toaster;
c) that the butter should be one-seventeenth the thickness of the bread.

WHAT'S IN A NAME?

The original meaning of a few place names:

Anguilla – eel
Annapurna – abundant food
Aran Islands – kidney islands
Bangkok – region of olive trees
Bethlehem – house of bread
Bethphage – house of figs
Chicago – garlic place
Clonmel – meadow of honey
Coney Island – rabbit island
Dalmatia – young animal
Danube – river of sheep
Fair Isle – islands of sheep
Galapagos – giant tortoise
Grasse – fat
Harbin – place where fish is dried
Killarney – church of the sloes
Saskatoon – fruit of tree of many branches
Shiraz – good grape
Topeka – a good place to dig potatoes

OLD PICTURE, NEW CAPTION

*Despite repeated attempts to be rid of them, the professor
realised he still had a mouse problem.*

FROM THE MOUTHS OF BABES

Advice for Kids was a popular round-robin email, immortalising the wisdom of some Australian pre-teens. Several (not surprisingly) involved food:

Never trust a dog to watch your food – Patrick, age 10
Never tell your mom her diet's not working – Michael, age 14
Stay away from prunes – Randy, age 9
You can't hide a piece of broccoli in a glass of milk – Armir, age 9
Puppies still have bad breath even after eating tic-tacs – Andrew, age 9
Don't sneeze in front of Mom when you're eating crackers –
Mitchell, age 12

TEN BAD MOMENTS IN A COOK'S LIFE

1. Seven ounces of flour left in the bag when you need eight
2. The lingering smell of fish in the room two days after a kedgeree
3. Not being sure whether the milk is off, and being torn between tasting it, going out to buy more or pouring it in to the ingredients and hoping for the best.
4. Lemon juice in a cut
5. A casserole dish fractionally too small for your leg of lamb
6. Waiting for a very large saucepan of water to boil
7. Finding nine promising ingredients in the cupboard, but realising that in no combination will they actually make a meal
8. Reading 'reserve the liquid' just after you've carefully strained said liquid down the sink
9. Finding only beef stock cubes when your guests are vegetarian, and wondering how bad it would be if…
10. Smoke alarms

A GANNET IS JUST FOR CHRISTMAS

For a few residents of the Outer Hebrides, Christmas dinner consists not of turkey, but of baby gannet. A local delicacy, it can be hard to come by, but once a year, the residents of Ness on the Isle of Lewis are allowed to cull a small number of young gannets for their festive dinner. The gannet, or 'guga', is eaten just with boiled potatoes, instead of all the trimmings that the rest of us expect. The flavour is described as being between that of a duck and a mackerel, with an oily skin (the gannet oozes black oil before it is cooked). To prepare a gannet, the cook must scrape off the salt covering with which it is sold, soak it overnight and boil it for 90 minutes, with several changes of water, during which process it reportedly smells absolutely terrible.

Bakewell Tart

The small Derbyshire town has a pudding named after it supposedly because of a hapless cook, although the story is thought to be more myth than fact. In the 18th century, the assistant cook at the Rutland Arms Hotel was making strawberry jam tarts as the dessert of the day. However she put jam at the bottom of the pastry case and then poured butter, eggs and sugar over the top and baked it all. Luckily, the guests loved the new dessert and the recipe has survived. Today, the treat comprises a sweet pastry base, with a red jam and almond filling, covered with a deep layer of white icing. A glacé cherry is then placed on top.

Bath Buns

The first Bath Bun is thought to have been served in the Pump Room in Bath during the 1670s. It is a round, yeasty cake flavoured with mixed spices and lemon and decorated with currants and nibbed sugar. It is baked on top of sugar cubes that soften during baking and are absorbed into the dough, leaving a pattern of neat squares on the bottom and a crunchy texture.

Battenburg Cake

Named in honour of the marriage of Princess Victoria to Prince Louis of Battenburg in 1884, this cake consists of four square lengths of sponge cake, baked in an oblong tin. Two of the lengths are pink and two are yellow and they are stuck together with apricot jam and wrapped in a layer of marzipan. It is still one of Britain's favourite cakes.

Black Forest Gateau

The Black Forest area in the south of Germany is known for the quality of its pastries, cakes, and especially for sour cherries and the cakes made from those cherries. Black Forest Gateau is chocolate cake with cherries and whipped cream.

Brussel Sprouts

The origin of the sprout is unknown but the first mention of them can be traced to the late 16th century. They are thought to be native to Belgium, especially to the area around Brussels, hence the name. They remained a local crop until they spread after the first world war and are now cultivated across Europe and the US. Their season is between August and March, perhaps accounting for their popularity on the dinner table on Christmas Day.

Cornish Pasties

The now famous Cornish pasty is attributed to the area from where it originated. The pasty originally came about as a handy lunch to be taken down the tin mines by local men. It was practical and yet hardy, the traditional filling being beef and potato, with some onion thrown in for good measure. This made a hearty meal and the pastry case kept it edible while the men were down the mines; and a knob of pastry at one end meant it could be held with dirty hands, then the lump discarded. Wives used to mark their husbands' initials into the pastry before it was cooked so they could identify theirs. Tradition has it that original pasties contained meat and vegetables in one end and jam or fruit in the other end, so there were two courses.

Coburg Loaf

Queen Victoria's consort, Prince Albert, was responsible for the naming of the Coburg Loaf. This is round and crusty with two slashes on the top. He came from Saxe-Coburg and the loaf was introduced shortly after his marriage to Victoria in 1840.

Madeira Cake

This is a simple plain sponge cake, which is often sprinkled with candied lemon peel halfway through baking. The name comes from the fact that it is usually served with a glass of madeira, a fortified Portuguese wine and named after the Portuguese island from where the dessert wine originated.

Seville Orange

The Seville orange is named after the area in which it grows in Spain. It is a bitter orange, and closer to the original fruit, rather than the modern varieties grown commercially. The sour taste of the Seville orange is attributed to the slight acidity of the orange's juice.

Tabasco Sauce

This hot sauce is made from red peppers, vinegar, water and salt and is aged in white oak barrels. It is named after the Tabasco River and the Tabasco State in Mexico, but not the Tabasco pepper, which it does not contain. It has a hot, spicy flavour and has proved popular around the world, being sold in 110 countries and packaged in 19 different languages.

Yorkshire Pudding

The traditional accompaniment to the Sunday roast was originally a 'dripping pudding' cooked in a tin under the rotating spit on which the beef was cooking so that the juices from the meat dripped onto it, adding to the flavour. This 'pudding' was originally served as a starter course; or as a main course in families who couldn't afford enough meat for everyone. However it was the 18th century cook, Hannah Glasse who first gave it the name Yorkshire Pudding.

A FINE MESS

It was for a mess of pottage – a dish of soupy food – that Esau sold his birthright to Jacob, and now the phrase stands for a cheap price paid for something worthwhile. As this suggests, 'mess' originally meant a serving of food, or a course of a meal. It also meant a group of four people sitting down to dine together, which gave rise to the military 'mess', where meals are eaten by the armed forces.

REASONS TO STAY HUNGRY

Nineteen phobias that might spoil your appetite:

Acerophobia – fear of sourness
Alektorophobia – fear of chickens
Alliumphobia – fear of garlic
Arachibutyrophobia – fear of peanut butter sticking to the roof
of your mouth
Carnophobia – fear of meat
Deipnophobia – fear of dining and dinner conversation
Dipsophobia – fear of drinking
Emetophobia – fear of vomiting
Geumatophobia – fear of taste
Hedonophobia – fear of pleasure
Icthyophobia – fear of fish
Lachanophobia – fear of vegetables
Mageirocophobia – fear of cooking
Olfactophobia – fear of smell
Ostraconophobia – fear of shellfish
Panophobia – fear of everything
Phagophobia – fear of swallowing
Pnigophobia – fear of choking
Sitophobia – fear of food

QUOTE UNQUOTE

*Americans can eat garbage, provided you sprinkle it liberally with
ketchup, mustard, chilli sauce, Tabasco sauce, cayenne pepper, or
any other condiment which destroys the original flavor of the dish.*
HENRY MILLER, US novelist

COOKS IN BOOKS

Recipe for cock ale
Take ten gallons of ale and a large cock, the older the better. Parboil
the cock, flea him and stamp him in a stone mortar until his bones are
broken. You must craw and gut him when you flea him. Put him into
two quarts of sack, and put to it three pounds of raisins of the sun
stoned, some blades of mace, and a few cloves. Put all these into a
canvas bag, and a little while before you find the ale has done working, put the ale and bag together into a vessel. In a week or nine days'
time, bottle it up, fill the bottles but just above the necks, and leave
the same to ripen as other ale.

Eliza Smith, *The Compleat Housewife*, 1727

OLD PICTURE, NEW CAPTION

*'It's the Cook,' gasped Charles. 'I've told her a hundred times
not to use those damned tabasco chillis.'*

RECORD BREAKERS

If you wonder whether your vegetable patch is up to scratch, take this
list with you when you next go a-weeding...

Longest beetroot: 5.504m (18ft, 0.6in), grown in the UK in 2002
Longest carrot: 335cm (132in), grown in the UK in 1987
Longest corn cob: 92cm (36.25ins) grown in the UK in 1994
Longest courgette: 1.34m (53in) grown in the USA in 2000
Longest cucumber: 1.1m (43.5in) grown in the UK in 1986
Longest parsnip: 5m (16ft, 4in) grown in the UK in 2000
Largest bunch of bananas: 473 bananas, grown in the Canary
Islands, 2001
Largest pumpkin: 606.7kg (1,337lb, 9oz), grown in the USA in 2002
Heaviest leek: 8.1kg (17lb, 13oz) grown in the UK in 2002
Tallest runner bean plant: 10.7m (35ft) grown in the UK in 1992

SAY IT WITH FOOD

Twelve ways to say that it's all gone horribly wrong

He's buttered his bread on both sides
He's been extravagant

He has need now of nothing but a little parsley
He's dead

It's neither fish, flesh nor good red herring
Not one thing or another, or not suitable for anything. These three foods were considered food for monks, food for everyone, and food for poor people respectively

It's not the cheese
It's not right; it doesn't cut the mustard

My cake is dough
My projects have failed

To be done brown
To be deceived

To eat the calf in the cow's belly To count your chickens before they're hatched

To pluck a pigeon
To take money off a gullible person

To shoe the goose
To waste time on pointless activities

The fat is in the fire
The cat's out of the bag

To take one's gruel
To accept one's punishment

Where the chicken got the axe
To get it in the neck

PLAYING WITH YOUR FOOD

Every year since 1999, the Yorkshire town of Brawby has held a Yorkshire Pudding race, for which participants must create a boat out of the ingredients of this traditional dish. Each boat requires around 50 eggs, four bags of flour and 25 pints of milk. The mixture is baked, lined with industrial foam-filler and made water-resistant with layers of yacht varnish.

The race was dreamed up by Simon Thackray, a local artist, who, while staring out of the window of his local pub one afternoon, mused: 'Wouldn't it be great to sail down a river in a giant Yorkshire pudding?' He created a small prototype from a shop-bought pudding, powered by a small electric motor, which had its maiden voyage in his bath. Despite the name, it is not so much a race as a display of creative endeavour and eccentricity. 'There is,' says Thackray, 'a start but no finish.'

The dying words of a few whose last thoughts turned to food...

'Be it so. But before I go, allow me to finish the remainder.'
Philoxenes of Cythera, Greek philosopher, when told the fish he was eating would kill him.

'May 4, 1823: No food for 71 days. I am the last one left alive.'
Final entry by **anonymous sailor** in the log book of the SS Jenny, lost at sea in 1823 and found preserved in ice in 1860.

'Let not poor Nelly starve.'
Charles II, died 1685, referring to his mistress Nell Gwynn.

'I beg a thousand pardons, my friend, but allow me to finish this last dozen oysters.'
Duc de Lanzon de Biron, French military commander, guillotined in 1793.

'I feel the end approaching. Quick, bring me my dessert, coffee, and liqueur.'
Jean-Anthelme Brillat-Savarin died 1826.

'I'll take a wee drop of that. I don't think there's much fear of me learning to drink now.'
James Croll, scientist and tee-totaller, died 1890.

'I should never have switched from Scotch to Martinis.'
The alleged last words of **Humphrey Bogart**, died 1957.

'The quenelles are good, only they were prepared too hastily; you must shake the saucepan lightly.'
Marie-Antoine Carême, died 1833 while tasting food in his kitchen.

'Bullets tipped with garlic.'
Johnny Torrio, US gangster, shot by his rivals in 1924.

'So might I safely swallow this morsel of bread, as I am guilt-less of the deed.'
Earl Godwin, Earl of the West-Saxons, accused by Edward the Confessor of murder. Died in 1053, choking on the piece of bread that he had to eat to prove his innocence.

'Don't let Day [the maid] eat all the Elvas plums.'
Margaret Jourdain, longtime companion of Ivy Compton-Burnett, died 1951

'That was the best ice-cream soda I ever tasted.'
Lou Costello, US comic actor, died 1959.

The trouble with eating Italian food is that five or six days later you're hungry again.
GEORGE MILLER, writer

SONGS WITH A LITTLE FLAVOUR

American Pie – Don MacLean
Banana Republic – Boomtown Rats
Big Apple – Kajagoogoo
Black Coffee – All Saints
Blueberry Hill – Fats Domino
Breakfast in America – Supertramp
Breakfast in Bed – UB40 with Chrissie Hynde
Brown Sugar – Rolling Stones
Butterfingers – Tommy Steele
Candy Girl – New Edition
Candy Man – Brian Poole and the Tremeloes
The Chicken Song – Spitting Image
Chocolate Salty Balls – Chef (from TV show *South Park*)
Cold Turkey – Plastic Ono Band
Cornflake Girl – Tori Amos
Does Your Chewing Gum Lose Its Flavour – Lonnie Donegan
Green Onions – Booker T and the MGs
I Eat Cannibals – Toto Coelo
I Heard It Through the Grapevine – Marvin Gaye
Judge Fudge – Happy Mondays
Life is a Minestrone – 10cc

FUEL FOR THE FIRE

The Great Fire of London took on a culinary theme when it was
alleged to have started in Master Farriner's bakery in Pudding Lane.
It began on Sunday morning, 2 September 1666, and within five
days had destroyed property over 460 acres, including 86 churches.
It was finally brought to a halt by the blowing up of houses at Pie
Corner in Smithfield.

EXPERT ADVICE

• To get more juice out of a lemon or lime, either bash and roll it
on the worktop before cutting and squeezing it, or microwave it
for 10-15 seconds before juicing
• If you're short of space and saucepans (and stamina) at a dinner
party, make the sauce ahead of time and keep it hot in a Thermos
flask.
• To stop okra going slimy, sharpen the stem end to a point, like a
pencil, before you cook it.
• If your pastry's a bit sticky or fragile, roll it out between two
sheets of floured baking parchment.

LITERARY FEASTS

Kant, the prince of German philosophers, who died in 1804, was not at all refined in his tastes; he took great pleasure in a purée of lentils, in a purée of parsnips cooked with pork fat; in a pudding of pork fat, Pomeranian style; in a pudding of dried peas with pigs' trotters, and in dried fruit baked in the oven. Kant considered three hours the right length of time in which to enjoy these various dishes, sitting down to eat at one o' clock and applying himself in a truly philosophical manner to this serious business until he rose at four.

P G Philomneste, *Le Livre des Singularités*

SPUD TROUBLE

The humble potato has caused a lot of bother throughout history...

The Swiss believed potatoes caused scrofula.

In 1774, the citizens of Kolberg refused to eat potatoes sent by Frederick the Great of Prussia to relieve their famine, until forced to do so by the militia.

Until 1780, potatoes were excluded from prudent French tables, as they were thought to cause leprosy.

Devout Scotch Presbyterians refused to eat them because they weren't mentioned in the Bible.

In Prussia, King Frederick William I threatened to cut off the noses and ears of any peasants who refused to plant them.

Russian peasants considered them unclean and un-Christian,

calling them 'Devil's apples'.

In colonial Massachusetts, they were considered the spoor of witches.

Ireland made the potato the foundation of its national diet; and act that was to have terrible repercussions in 1845 when a late blight attacked the potato crop and caused a devastating famine in which over a million people died.

In 2001, Indian vegetarian lawyer Harish Bharti attempted to sue McDonald's, the omnipresent burger chain. Bharti claimed that McDonald's had misled its customers by announcing in 1990 that its fries would from that day on be cooked in 100% vegetable oil, but omitting to mention that they later added beef flavouring.

COOKING CONUNDRUMS

Who is the larger: Methuselah, Salmanazar or Balthazar?
Answer on page 153

SO THAT'S WHAT THEY MEAN BY HIGH TABLE

The highest formal meal eaten was served at 6,768m (22,205ft) at the top of Mount Huascaran in Peru on 28 June 1989. Nine members of the Ansett Social Climbers from Sydney scaled the mountain with a Louis XIV dining table, chairs, silverware, candelabra, wine and a three-course meal.

FAMOUS COOKS

Peter Cook – writer, actor, comedian and the founder of *Private Eye*. Genius or madman, depending on your sense of humour.

Captain James Cook – 18th century navigator and explorer and the author of three books about his voyages to the Pacific Ocean, during which the main shorelines were discovered.

Thomas Cook – born in Derbyshire, the future travel agent started life as a Baptist missionary. He became involved in the travel business after an excursion to Loughborough for a temperance meeting led to Cook arranging the first public train excursion. He soon branched out into European train trips to become the huge international travel agent that it is today.

Alistair Cooke – journalist and broadcaster. He was famous for his *Letter from America*, which was broadcast by the BBC from 1946 until 2004. This made his radio programme the longest-running solo radio feature programme.

Robin Cook – a Labour Party politician who resigned his position as Leader of the House of Commons and Lord President of the Council in March 2003 over the British government's involvement in the conflict with Iraq. He had been foreign secretary from 1997 to 2001.

Norman Cook – otherwise known as Fatboy Slim the dance music producer and DJ. He first shot to fame in the mid 1980s with the Housemartins. He is now known both for his successful music and his marriage to former Radio 1 DJ and television presenter Zoë Ball.

Beryl Cook – British artist who paints distinctively overweight and jovial characters. Her work is suggestive of saucy postcard humour and has been widely used on greeting cards.

Sam Cook – a famous soul singer of the 1960s who was was involved in the civil rights movement in the US. He was murdered in 1964 by an LA hotel manager.

WORLD'S LARGEST FOOD FIGHT

The fruity festival of La Tomatina is a week-long celebration with bonfires, fireworks, drinking and entertainment to honour Saint Louis, the patron saint of the town of Bunol near Valencia. In 2001, 38,000 people spent an hour throwing 120 tonnes of tomatoes at each other. At the end, the town is awash with tomato juice and squashed tomatoes. It takes place on the last Wednesday of August – and as if that weren't enough food, the night before is usually marked by a giant paella cook-off.

TASTY CHILDHOOD TALES

The Adventures of Huckleberry Finn, Mark Twain
The Battle of Bubble and Squeak, Philippa Pearce
Charlie and the Chocolate Factory, Roald Dahl
The Chocolate War, Robert Cormier
Each Peach Pear Plum, Janet and Allan Ahlberg
The Great Big Enormous Turnip, Helen Oxenbury
Green Eggs and Ham, Dr Seuss
Garth Pig and the Ice Cream Lady, Mary Rayner
I Am The Cheese, Robert Cormier
James and the Giant Peach, Roald Dahl
Orlando the Marmalade Cat, Kathleen Hale
Peacock Pie, Walter de la Mare
The Peppermint Pig, Nina Bawden
The Piemakers, Helen Cresswell
The Story of Chicken Licken, traditional fairy tale
The Tale of the Pie and the Patty-Pan, Beatrix Potter
The Tale of Ginger and Pickles, Beatrix Potter
Cecily Parsley's Nursery Rhymes, Beatrix Potter

LITERARY FEASTS

Tidmouth: A sandwich, I mean. I'm having one. I say, these are extraordinarily good. Sardine, or my senses deceive me. (*He tests this theory by taking another, and all doubts are removed.*) Yes, absolutely sardine. I read an interesting thing in the paper the other day. It said the sardine's worst enemy was the halibut, and I give you my word that until I read it I didn't even know the sardine had an enemy. And I don't mind telling you my opinion of the halibut has gone down considerably. Very considerably. Fancy anything wanting to bully a sardine.

PG Wodehouse, *Good Morning, Bill,* Act One

I'LL HAVE WHAT SHE'S HAVING

Futterneid is German for 'food envy' – that feeling you get when the main course arrives and you wish you'd ordered what your friend ordered.

WHY ENGINEERS DON'T WRITE RECIPE BOOKS

In 2003, this ingenious gem was circulated on the internet, and is reproduced here as evidence that there are some engineers out there with a fine sense of humour.

Chocolate Chip Cookies
Ingredients:
1. 532.35 cm3 gluten
2. 4.9 cm3 NaHCO3
3. 4.9 cm3 refined halite
4. 236.6 cm3 partially hydrogenated tallow triglyceride
5. 177.45 cm3 crystalline C12H22O11
6. 177.45 cm3 unrefined C12H22O11
7. 4.9 cm3 methyl ether of protocatechuic aldehyde
8. Two calcium carbonate-encapsulated avian albumen-coated protein
9. 473.2 cm3 theobroma cacao
10. 236.6 cm3 de-encapsulated legume meats (sieve size #10)

To a 2-L jacketed round reactor vessel (reactor #1) with an overall heat transfer coefficient of about 100 Btu/F-ft2-hr, add ingredients one, two and three with constant agitation. In a second 2-L reactor vessel with a radial flow impeller operating at 100 rpm, add ingredients four, five, six, and seven until the mixture is homogenous. To reactor #2, add ingredient eight, followed by three equal volumes of the homogenous mixture in reactor #1. Additionally, add ingredient nine and 10 slowly, with constant agitation. Care must be taken at this point in the reaction to control any temperature rise that may be the result of an exothermic reaction.

Using a screw extrude attached to a #4 nodulizer, place the mixture piece-meal on a 316SS sheet (300 x 600 mm). Heat in a 460K oven for a period of time that is in agreement with Frank & Johnston's first order rate expression (see JACOS, 21, 55), or until golden brown. Once the reaction is complete, place the sheet on a 25C heat-transfer table, allowing the product to come to equilibrium.

CHINESE YORKSHIRE PUDDING

On 25 April 1970, the city of Leeds held a competition to discover Britain's best Yorkshire pudding maker. Three English hotel chefs, a Leeds University student and a housewife were humbled by Hong Kong-born Tin Sung Chan, a Chinese chef, who won first prize.

Asked the secret of his success, Chan, chef at the Chopsticks Restaurant, said 'I put in a secret ingredient. It's a Chinese herb called tai luk.' The judges didn't know what it was, but they must have liked it. *The Guardian* reported that his pudding 'rose to the height of a coronation crown and its taste, according to one of the judges, was superb.' Chan won a holiday in Ireland.

COOKING CONUNDRUMS

Why is gooseberry fool called a fool?
Answer on page 153

THE INVENTIONS THAT TIME FORGOT

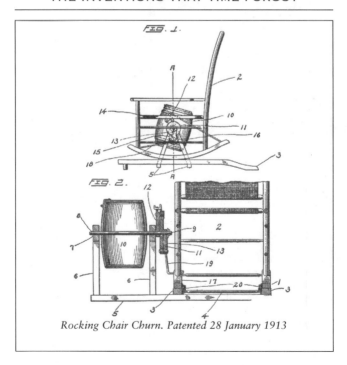

Rocking Chair Churn. Patented 28 January 1913

COOKS IN BOOKS

Clémentine in the kitchen! The bright-eyed little cook brought new significance to that part of the house, which had waited so long for a presiding genius. It was a neat and ample kitchen. Its red tile floor was worn down in spots but always beautifully waxed. Above the stove was our pride and joy, a shimmering *batterie de cuisine*, fourteen heavy copper pans, polished and tin-lined, hanging against the wall in mathematical progression. They ranged from a huge fellow big enough to roast a duck to the tiny vessel just about right for poaching an egg. There was an efficient stove, a commodious and rather ancient soapstone sink, a shelf for a library of cookbooks, from Tante-Marie to Ali Bab, a massive oak chopping-board, and some well-balanced scales with a squad of neat little metric weights. A white marble-topped table stood in the middle of the kitchen, its drawer crammed with sauce whisks, wooden spoons, and a murderous collection of sharp steel knives. In a low cupboard was a mighty assemblage of seasoned earthen casseroles, some with handles, some with covers that could be hermetically sealed. On top of the cupboard was a husky stone mortar with a dark wooden pestle. Hanging near the door were the two invariable adjuncts of a French kitchen – a salad basket and a birdcage.

Samuel Chamberlain, *Clémentine in the Kitchen*, 1943

FOOD FOR THOUGHT

• In 2000, the food industry spent around £10.9 billion on chemical food additives to improve the colour, flavour, texture and shelf life of its products.

• Consumers in the developed world ingest between six and seven kilogrammes of food additives a year.

• Some of these additives are designed to prevent food poisoning and prolong the life of the food. However, the additives that prevent food from deteriorating account for only 1% of all additives in food. Around 90% are used for cosmetic reasons, to change the colour, flavour or texture of the food.

• There are 540 food additive compounds that are deemed safe for human consumption by regulatory bodies.

• Of the 540, 320 are accepted as reasonably safe. Doubts have been raised about the safety of 150 others. Seventy may cause allergic reactions and intolerance in some people and 30 could cause significant long-term damage to consumers.

• Only seven pesticides are allowed in organic food, all of which are non-synthetic.

THE FOOD OF LOVE

The word 'aphrodisiac' comes from the name of the goddess of love, Aphrodite, although it is more commonly thought of as something that provokes lust rather than love. Whatever effect you're looking for, here are a few traditional favourites:

Asparagus has that all-important phallic shape, but is also rich in vitamin E, a vitamin that is believed by some to stimulate production of our sex hormones and to be essential for a healthy sex life.

The heat in **chilli peppers** comes from capsaicin, a chemical that stimulates our nerve endings, raising our pulse, making us sweat and simulating a state of sexual arousal. Some researchers believe that eating hot foods also triggers the release of endorphins, chemicals that give us a natural high that is similar to, and conducive to, love-making.

Chocolate contains a stimulant called phenylethylamine, which creates a feeling of well-being and excitement similar to that experienced when making love. It also contains two stimulants, theobromine and caffeine. Research suggests that the amounts of all of these in chocolate are too low to make a difference. We say that the gift of a pound of Belgian truffles can provoke all kinds of interesting emotions.

Coffee contains caffeine, a stimulant. Also, sperm exposed to caffeine swim faster. However, in past eras, caffeine was thought to deprive the body of semen and render a man impotent.

Damiana, or wild yam, has traditionally been used as an aphrodisiac, and chemical analysis shows that it contains chemicals that can increase sensitivity in the genitals. It is also used as an alternative remedy for hormone replacement, as it is believed to affect hormone levels in the body.

Some experimenters have used **gingko** successfully to treat sexual dysfunction, possibly because it stimulates the release of nitric oxide. This widens the blood vessels of the genitals and erectile tissue, which sounds effective, if unromantic.

Research shows that **oysters** are rich in zinc, a mineral required for the production of testosterone. Testosterone is believed to stimulate the female libido as well as the male. The texture and taste are also supposed to have something to do with the oyster's aphrodisiac effect, via the imagination.

Although there is no scientific background, it is thought that the pungent aroma of a **truffle** and its exciting rarity help to create a degree of stimulation. As Brillat-Savarin wrote: 'The truffle is not a true aphrodisiac, but in certain circumstances it can make women more affectionate and men more attentive.'

MORE SONGS WITH A LITTLE FLAVOUR

Marguerita Time – Status Quo
Milk and Alcohol – Dr Feelgood
Mistletoe and Wine – Cliff Richard
Money Honey – Bay City Rollers
Monster Mash – Bobby Pickett and the Crypt Kickers
Mouldy Old Dough – Lieutenant Pigeon
My Boy Lollipop – Millie
My Girl Lollipop – Bad Manners
No Milk Today – Herman's Hermits
Peaches – Stranglers
Red Red Wine – UB40
Strawberry Fields For Ever – The Beatles
Sugar and Spice – The Searchers
Sugar Baby Love – Rubettes
Sugar Town – Nancy Sinatra
Sweet Like Chocolate – Shanks and Bigfoot
Sweets for My Sweet – The Searchers
2 Pints of Lager and a Packet of Crisps Please – Splodgenessabounds
Whiskey in the Jar – Thin Lizzy

QUOTE UNQUOTE

He was a bold man that first ate an oyster.
JONATHAN SWIFT, writer

CULINARY LEGENDS

Georges Auguste Escoffier (1846-1935), French chef *extraordinaire* was renowned for his superb cooking, the prestige of his patrons, his modernising influence on hotel cooking, in particular at the London Savoy, and the sheer length of his culinary career. Escoffier was chef at the Carlton Hotel in London, the Grande National Hotel in Lucerne, Switzerland, the Grand Hotel in Monte Carlo, the Savoy in London and the Ritz hotels in Paris and New York City. He wrote many authoritative books about cooking, and was made a Chevalier of the Legion of Honour in 1920. Emperor William II summed up Escoffier's career with the words: 'I am the Emperor of Germany, but you are the emperor of chefs.'

IT MUST HAVE BEEN SOMETHING THEY ATE

The number of reported cases of food poisoning in the UK rose from 59,721 in 1990 to 98,076 in 2000.

BIG EATERS

The largest item to be found on any menu is probably a roasted camel, which occasionally graces a Bedouin wedding feast. The whole dish consists of cooked eggs stuffed into fish, stuffed into a cooked chicken, which is stuffed into a roasted sheep's carcass, which is, finally, stuffed into the camel. A modern equivalent might be the Turducken, invented by a Louisiana chef in the 1960s; a chicken, duck and turkey are boned and laid out flat, with the turkey on the outside, then the duck and the chicken on top. All three birds are rolled up and sewn in place, and the whole is roasted slowly for up to 13 hours.

SOMEONE TO WATCH OVER YOU

There are patron saints for everything, it seems, and food is no exception:

Adrian of Nicomedia – butchers
Anthony of Padua – against starvation
Pascal Baylon – cooks, especially New Mexican cooking
Charles Borromeo – apple orchards
Bridgid of Ireland – dairy workers
Drogo – coffee house owners
Erasmus – against abdominal pain
Elizabeth of Hungary – bakers
Honoratus – bakers, cake makers
Honorius of Amiens – confectioners
Joseph – confectioners
Lawrence – butchers, confectioners,
cooks, restaurateurs, brewers and wine makers
Macarius the Younger – pastry cooks
Martha – cooks
Michael – grocery stores
Nicholas of Myra – bakers
Urban – wine
Walburga – against famine

PEASE PORRIDGE NINE DAYS OLD

Centuries ago, people used to cook in a big pot that always hung over the fire. Every day they lit the fire and added things to the pot. Meat was hard to come by and the main ingredient was vegetables. They would eat the stew for dinner, leaving leftovers in the pot and then heat them up again the next day. Sometimes the stew had food in it that had been there for quite a while – hence the rhyme, 'Pease porridge hot, pease porridge cold, pease porridge in the pot nine days old.'

ALL I WANT FOR CHRISTMAS

According to a BBC programme broadcast in December 2003, this is what the British insist on at Christmas, in order of priority:

1. Turkey and all the trimmings
2. Christmas pudding
3. Sherry trifle
4. Mince pies
5. Roast chicken
6. Baked glazed ham
7. Christmas cake
8. Smoked salmon
9. Turkey sandwiches
10. Roast goose
11. Nut roast

But what did the experts think?

Turkey: 'We eat turkey because it's the biggest thing we can kill. Size matters' – Nigel Slater

Christmas pudding: 'It shouldn't resemble a light sponge. It should be like a cannonball' – Keith Floyd

Sherry trifle: 'It's got all the things childhood is made of and then because you're grown-up you add alcohol' – Clarissa Dickson-Wright

Mince pies: 'Mince pies are the thing to get plastered with after midnight mass' – Anthony Worrall-Thompson

Roast chicken: 'Who the hell would want to eat roast chicken on Christmas Day?' – Gordon Ramsay

Baked ham: 'Go for the pig's left leg, because it's more tender, as pigs scratch with their right, so that leg is more muscular' – narrator's advice.

Christmas cake: 'It's good to have a bit of Christmas cake to lift your blood sugar when you're running around playing silly games and having too much sex' – Clarissa Dickson-Wright

Smoked salmon: 'It's that feeling of luxury. Even if you eat it as often as I do, it's still a treat' – Clarissa Dickson-Wright

Turkey sandwiches: 'There's no such thing as a good turkey sandwich' – Keith Floyd

Roast goose: 'It should be number one. Comparing a goose to a turkey is like comparing a Bentley Turbo and a Ford Fiesta' – Keith Floyd

Nut roast: 'Vegetarians deserve better' – Nigel Slater

QUOTE UNQUOTE

The most dangerous food is wedding cake.
JAMES THURBER, US writer and cartoonist

ELEVEN REPETITIVE FOODS

agar-agar – a vegetarian alternative to gelatine, made from seaweed
al pil-pil – in Spain, anything cooked in an olive oil and garlic sauce
alfalfa – when sprouted from seed, a delicate salad vegetable
baba – cake made from leavened dough that is steeped in
rum after baking
coco – plum-like fruit from West Indies and Central America
couscous – small grain made of wheat or barley
fufu – also called foufou, a starchy African savoury
pudding or thick porridge
pawpaw – another name for papaya
pili-pili – a small, hot African pepper
quinquina – a bitter wine-based aperitif containing quinine
tartar – crystalline deposit left inside wine casks, which when
purified is used in baking as cream of tartar

EXPERT ADVICE

The secret to perfect fluff

To make sure egg whites go fluffy when you beat them, make sure
the bowl and utensils are very clean and absolutely bone-dry. Use a
glass, ceramic, stainless steel or copper bowl. Don't use a plastic
bowl, as you can't be sure it is spotlessly clean and dry – grease can
hide in even small scratches on the surface. A copper bowl is best,
as the reaction of egg white and copper makes them lighter, but
don't leave them to rest too long in the bowl after beating.

Bring the egg whites to room temperature before you whisk; the
colder they are, the longer they take to go fluffy. Use a large bowl to
give plenty of room, and a large balloon whisk. If you use an
electric mixer, start slowly until the whites turn to foam, then speed
up to finish them off. And don't overwhisk, or the foam will
collapse and can't be rescued.

IN LOVING MEMORY

The Alferd Packer Memorial Grill in the University of Colorado was
named not after a generous benefactor, nor after an accomplished
chef, but after a local murderer who ate his victims. Alferd Packer
was a prospector who lived in the Rocky Mountains who split open
the skulls of his companions while they slept and ate their remains.
Caught in 1874 he was convicted and jailed for 18 years. However,
his story made him notorious rather than reviled, and he found
himself almost a curiosity on his release. Tourists still visit his grave
and students with strong stomachs named their refectory after him.

THE ORIGINS OF BREAD AND BUTTER

Between 5,000 and 12,000 years ago, man stopped chasing his food and began to herd and farm instead. Climatic changes at the end of the Ice Age encouraged more edible plants such as wheat to grow. As man learned to harvest food, and replant the seeds, he was able to settle in one place and build a home, as well as develop his cooking skills. As raw wheat is indigestible, historians conclude that at first it was roasted, ground, mixed with water and made into cakes on hot stones, somewhere around 9000 BC. These 'flatbreads' survive in various forms today in most cultures: pitta, nan, lavash, tortilla, chapatti and so on. And because man was still thinking about inventing pottery, it was the perfect food, as it could be made and eaten without containers or cutlery.

In the Middle Ages, trencher bread was used to make a plate for meat dishes, then the soggy remains were given to the dogs, or to the poor.

But what to put on the bread? Between 9000 BC and 6000 BC, man began to domesticate animals, starting with goats and sheep. This gave him meat and milk as well as wool, skin, leather, fat, dung and bones. As with flatbreads, milk in its natural and fermented state is still a part of almost every traditional diet, from yogurt to Indian dahi and the 'discovery' of milk was closely followed by the invention of butter. Incidentally, it is thought that the use of animal stomachs as containers for milk probably created the first cheese, as the rennet in a calf's stomach helps to make milk into cheese.

SAFETY AT HOME

These are the most common causes of domestic fires in homes in the UK. More than one household in 100 experiences a pan catching fire.

Pan of fat or oil catching fire	24%
Grill pan catching fire	13%
Leaving something in or on the cooker for too long	7%
Arson	6%
Leaving something too close to the cooker	5%
Candles	5%
Chimney fires	5%
Toaster	4%
Electric wiring worn out or faulty	3%
Microwave	2%
Cigar/cigarette	2%

• The word coffee comes from the Arabic, *qahwah*, a poetic word for wine. Coffee was first made from boiling the leaves, rather than roasting and grinding the beans. The first person to make coffee from beans is believed to have been an Islamic hermit called ad-Shadhili, around 1200 AD, in north Africa. In Algeria, you can still ask for a cup of *al-shadhili* instead of coffee.

• Islamic alchemists believed that mixing coffee with milk caused leprosy.

• The coffee we buy is mostly either robusta or arabica. Arabica is considered a better quality; a mixture of robusta and arabica is sufficient for everyday use.

• Coffee beans were first brought to Europe in 1615, by the Italians.

• The first coffee house in Europe was opened by a Turkish Jew, in Oxford, in 1650. The first coffee-house in London was opened in St Michael's Alley in Cornhill in 1652.

• Hazrat Shah Jamer Allah Mazarabi smuggled seven green coffee beans out of Mecca, taped to his stomach, and took them to India. Taking 'live' beans out of the country was punishable by death. He planted them in Mysore, and single-handedly began the entire Indian coffee-producing industry. A seedling was taken from this plantation to Indonesia in 1696 by a Dutchman, which in turn began the long history of Indonesian coffee plantations of the 18th century.

• In Italy, coffee is sometimes drunk with a curl of lemon peel, sprinkling of grated lemon or orange peel; in Russia with a squeeze of lemon juice; in Morocco with whole black peppercorns; in Ethiopia and Morocco with a pinch of salt; in France with a dash of any spirit or liqueur; and in Normandy half and half with Calvados.

• The first International Coffee Agreement took place at the United Nations in 1962. It was intended to balance out supply and demand and ensure fair pricing. The last such agreement expired in 1989.

• The National Institute on Drug Abuse claimed that, in the last recorded year, 5,000 Americans were killed by caffeine in one year. By contrast, 125,000 were killed by alcohol, and none were killed by marijuana.

• Cafédirect coffee was one of the first three products to be sold through the Fairtrade scheme. Fairtrade coffee now accounts for 18% of UK roast and ground coffee.

LITERARY FEASTS

The railway station at Rome has put on a new face. Blown to the winds is that old dignity and sense of leisure… That restaurant for example – one of those few for which a man in olden days of peace would desert his own tavern in the town – how changed! The fare has deteriorated beyond recognition. Where are those succulent joints and ragouts, the aromatic wine, the snow-white macaroni, the café-au-lait with genuine butter and genuine honey?

War-time!

Conversed awhile with an Englishman at my side, who was gleefully devouring lumps of a particular something which I would not have liked to touch with tongs.

'I don't care what I eat,' he remarked.

So it seemed.

I don't care what I eat: what a confession to make! Is it not the same thing as saying, I don't care whether I am dirty or clean? When others tell me this, I regard it as a pose, or a poor joke. This person was manifestly sincere in his profession of faith. He did not care what he ate. He looked it. Were I afflicted with this particular ailment, this attenuated form of coprophagia, I should try to keep the hideous secret to myself. It is nothing to boast of. A man owes something to those traditions of our race which have helped to raise us above the level of the brute. Good taste in viands has been painfully acquired; it is a sacred trust. Beware of gross feeders. They are a menace to their fellow-creatures.

Norman Douglas, *Alone*

OLD PICTURE, NEW CAPTION

*Dr Prendergast demonstrates the benefits
of a vitamin-enriched diet*

THAT'S WHY THE COOKIE CRUMBLES

A student from Loughborough University claimed in 2003 to have found the reason why so many biscuits are broken before the packet is opened. While customers assume it is due to rough handling by shop staff, PhD student Qasim Salim thought otherwise and set out to prove a theory. He baked over 100 biscuits during his research, and measured them with laser technology known as digital speckle pattern interferometry. He concluded that when a biscuit cools, it accumulates moisture around the rim, which causes it to expand, but at the same time it loses moisture at the centre, which makes it contract. The opposing forces cause the biscuit to crack. Salim's research supervisor claimed that the findings could be extremely valuable to the £1.5 billion biscuit industry, by reducing waste.

BEFORE THEY WERE FAMOUS

Some early occupations of well-known people:

Robert Burns – farmer
Michael Caine – Billingsgate fish porter
Jimmy Carter – peanut farmer
Frank Finlay – butcher
Benny Hill – milkman
Ho Chi Minh – hotel worker and pastry cook
Bob Hoskins – market porter
Magnus Pyke – nutritionist
Jimmy Tarbuck – milkman
Tennessee Williams – waiter

A MATTER OF TASTE

If you thought that all you could taste was sweet, sour, salty and bitter, rejoice – there is another taste to savour, known as *umami*. In 1908, Professor Ikeda from the University of Tokyo set out to find what made *kombu*, the traditional Japanese seaweed broth, taste so delicious. He narrowed it down to glutamic acid, or glutamate, which gives food a rich, savoury taste best described as mouthfulness. Ikeda called it *umami*, which roughly translated means 'deliciousness'. Parmesan is very high in glutamate, for example, as are sundried tomatoes and tomato paste. As other scientists became interested, they discovered more substances that gave foods a hint of *umami*, and these were found in foods such as dried bonito flakes, shiitake mushrooms, fish sauce, meat and vegetable extracts such as Marmite, soy sauce and many other fermented products. So the next time you eat something divinely delicious, remember – it's probably the glutamates.

BUG CLUB

For those whose meals lack that essential crunch, Iowa State University has an Entomology Club, which offers a batch of tasty insect recipes, available on the internet, for such delicacies as Bug Blox, Banana Worm Bread, Rootworm Beetle Dip, Chocolate Chirpie Chip Cookies, Crackers and Cheese Dip with Candied Crickets, Mealworm Fried Rice, Corn Borer Cornbread Muffins and Chocolate-covered Grasshoppers. They also helpfully provide a nutritional chart (a dung beetle contains 17.2g protein, for example, and crickets are surprisingly high in calcium) as well as links to insect cookbooks and where to buy your insects.

To celebrate their unusual culinary habits, every year the Entomology Club hosts an Insect Horror Film Festival, featuring gourmet insect tasting, live insect displays, a butterfly house, informational displays, and a classic insect movie.

WHAT'S THE DIFFERENCE?

A conserve is much more than mere strawberry jam:

Conserves: Like jam, containing whole or pieces of fruit, but with a slightly softer set

Fruit butter: Thick preserve made from fruit purée and sugar, often with spices added

Fruit cheese: Made as fruit butter but cooked to a thick, firm consistency

Fruit curd: Fruit juice and zest mixed with sugar, butter and eggs

Jam: Made from fruit pulp or pieces, and a syrup made with the fruit juice and sugar

Jellies: Clear preserve made from the strained juice of cooked fruit, with sugar added

Marmalades: Jam made with citrus fruit and containing pieces of peel

COOKS IN BOOKS

What shall I tell you, my lady, of the secrets of nature I have learned while cooking?... One can philosophise quite well while preparing supper. I often say, when I have these little thoughts, 'Had Aristotle cooked, he would have written a great deal more.'

Juana Ines de la Cruz, *Epistola a Filotea*

CULINARY LEGENDS

Jean Anthelme Brillat-Savarin (1775-1826) is perhaps France's best-known gastronome, a lawyer and magistrate who wrote one of the most celebrated works on food, *Physiologie du Gout* (The Physiology of Taste), published in 1825. He gained a love of food from his mother, an accomplished *cordon bleu* cook, but chose law as his profession, although he also studied medicine and chemistry. Appointed to the Supreme Court of Justice, he spent his leisure time writing treatises on various subjects, including food, and through his writing pursued his personal ambition to make the culinary arts a true science. His best-known work consists of eight volumes and its full title in English is *The Physiology of Taste, or Meditation on Transcendent Gastronomy, a Work Theoretical, Historical, and Programmed.* The work combines science and history with gastronomic meditations on such subjects as digestion, rest, sleep, obesity and thinness, the pleasures of the table, gourmands, appetite, fasting, death and the theory of frying.

QUOTE UNQUOTE

Gelée of duck has the consistency of Pamela Anderson Lee's implants, and was so salty and horrid it was like licking an Abyssinian shotputter's armpit.
AA GILL, writer and critic

TEN CARROT FACTS

1. Carrots were first grown as a medicine

2. Carrots were originally purple, red, white, black and yellow

3. Carrots were imported to Europe in the 14th century; Flemish refugees brought them to the UK in the 15th century

4. Orange carrots were bred by the Dutch to match the colours of the House of Orange

5. In James I's time, fashionable ladies wore the flowers and feathery leaves of the carrot in their hair as a decoration

6. Carrot tea made from the leaves is said to be good for gout

7. During World War II, carrots were used to make marmalade and fizzy drinks

8. Jelly beans are made in carrot pie flavour

9. There is as much carrot in four organic carrots as there is in five non-organic carrots

10. Mel Blanc, the voice of Bugs Bunny, didn't like carrots

AVOCADO AMMUNITION

In a letter to *The Times*, 11 May 1989...

Sir – In paying tribute to the versatility of the avocado pear, your recent correspondents appear to have overlooked its military applications.

When I was employed in the Colonial Secretariat in Entebbe 30 years ago, there was a fruitful avocado tree in our garden, windfalls from which provided an arsenal of ammunition for the rival gangs in which our own children and those of our colleagues used to play in their games. Indeed the gang based on the other side of our garden fence was fittingly known and respected as the Mighty Pear-Balls.

The over-ripe, rotten avocado pear is singularly well adapted for use as a projectile in juvenile gang warfare. It is not lethal; it is exactly the right size and weight for throwing; its large stone provides the requisite solidity and mass; and in the event of a direct hit its explosive potential is spectacularly satisfying.

Yours faithfully,
John Champion

JUST TIN TIME

The first tin opener was invented in 1855 – 45 years after the tin was invented.

MORE FILMS FOR FOODIES

The Atomic Café
Attack on a Bakery
The Breakfast Club
Breakfast in Bed
The Butcher's Wife
The Cook, The Thief, His Wife and Her Lover
Diner
Eat Drink Man Woman
Gas, Food, Lodging
The Man Who Came to Dinner
Naked Lunch
The Ploughman's Lunch
Steaming

COOKING CONUNDRUMS

In France, what does AAAAA stand for?
Answer on page 153

In a 2003 survey of eating habits in the UK, volunteers aged 19-64 recorded their regular food intake. The results are not entirely surprising, but dieticians of a sensitive nature may want to look away now.

Number who own a freezer	95%
Number who own a microwave	91%
Number who are currently on a diet	10% men 24% women
Number who are vegetarian or vegan	2% men 7% women

Percentage who ate the following foods at least once a week:

	Men	Women
white bread	93	89
biscuits	63	68
vegetables	81	80
chicken/turkey	82	77
bacon/ham	77	64
cheese	78	73
wholemeal bread	33	39
bananas	49	56
apples/pears	49	54
citrus fruits	25	30
table sugar	60	48
chocolate	54	57
other confectionery	20	25
soft drinks	52	48
beer	66	24
wine	36	45
tea	77	77
coffee	72	70

Portions of fruit and vegetables eaten per day: men 2.7, women 2.9

Number who eat five portions of fruit and vegetables per day: men 13% women 15%

Men aged 19-24 who eat three or more portions of fruit and veg per day: 0%

Overall, men and women aged 19-24 were more likely than those aged 50-64 to have eaten breaded chicken pieces, burgers, kebabs, savoury snacks, pasta, pizza, chips, fizzy drinks and alco-pops, and less likely to have eaten fresh vegetables and fruit, wholemeal bread, wholegrain cereals, eggs and oily fish.

Those on a lower income ate a smaller range of foods, fewer wholegrain and low-fat foods, fewer fruits and vegetables, more sugar and more ready-prepared meat products such as pies and kebabs.

LUCKY FOOD

A few Japanese superstitions

Do not pass food from chopstick to chopstick; this is only done with the bones of the cremated body at funerals.

Do not stick your chopsticks into your food, especially not into rice, because at funerals chopsticks are stuck into the rice that is put onto the altar.

Do not lie down after eating: if you lie down immediately after eating, you will become a cow.

NOW PLEASE WASH YOUR HANDS

US cook Mary Mallon (1870-1938) is better known as Typhoid Mary, the first typhoid carrier to be identified in the US. Though immune to the disease herself, she was believed to have caused 51 cases of typhoid and three deaths by passing the disease on. She was forcibly isolated in a New York hospital from 1907-1910, and released only on the condition that she did not work as a cook. However, when typhoid broke out at two hospitals, she was found to be working in the kitchens and was isolated in hospital for the rest of her life.

SAY IT WITH FOOD

Nine ways to insult someone in a foodie kind of way:

Every bean has its black – everyone has their faults, a reference to black-eyed beans

It seems beans are in flower – said to someone behaving in a silly fashion; it was once thought that the perfume of beans made people light-headed and nonsensical

Cheese it – stop it, or clear off

You're a loose fish – a person of dissolute habits. Fish is generally derogatory – a poor fish, a queer fish, a wet fish, a cold fish...

You drive your hog to market – you snore (loudly)

You have brought your hogs to a fine market – this is fine mess you've got yourself into

He's hog-shearing – he's making much ado about nothing

He's gone hog-wild – he's gone crazy

He died for want of lobster sauce – said of someone who suffers for want of something trifling (from a chef who killed himself when his lobster sauce did not arrive for a feast given for Louis XIV)

TOP TEN PASTAS

The UK's favourite pasta shapes in order of market share:

Spaghetti – 26%	Tagliatelle – 8.0%
Twists – 18%	Noodles – 7.1%
Assorted shapes – 13.5%	Macaroni – 6.3%
Lasagne – 9.2%	Tortellini – 2.5%
Shells – 9.0%	Cannelloni – 0.4%

I'LL EAT MY HATTE

The origin of this phrase has nothing, in fact, to do with headgear. Hattes have been found in early European cookbooks, although their ingredients and preparation are disputed. The acknowledged recipe included eggs, veal, dates, saffron and salt but could also include tongue, kidney, fat, honey, rosemary and cinnamon. It was generally thought to be an unappetising dish, and so the promise by someone that they would eat a hatte if they were wrong showed how sure they were that they would be proven right.

LITERARY FEASTS

I have been assured by a very knowing American of my Acquaintance in London; that a young healthy Child, well nursed, is, at a Year old, a most delicious, nourishing, and wholesome Food, whether Stewed, Roasted, Baked, or Boiled; and, I make no doubt, that it will equally serve in a Fricasie, or Ragoust.

I do therefore humbly offer it to publick Consideration, that of the Hundred and Twenty Thousand Children, already computed, Twenty thousand may be reserved for Breed... That the remaining Hundred thousand, may, at a Year old, be offered in Sale to the Persons of Quality and Fortune, through the Kingdom; always advising the Mother to let them suck plentifully in the last Month, so as to render them plump, and fat for a good Table. A Child will make two Dishes at an Entertainment for Friends; and when the Family dines alone, the fore or hind Quarter will make a reasonable Dish; and seasoned with a little Pepper or Salt, will be very good Boiled on the fourth Day, especially in Winter.

I have reckoned upon a Medium, that a Child just born will weigh Twelve Pounds; and in a solar Year, if tolerably nursed, encreaseth to twenty eight Pounds.

I grant this Food will be somewhat dear, and therefore very proper for Landlords; who, as they have already devoured most of the Parents, seem to have the best Title to the Children.

Jonathan Swift, *A Modest Proposal*

What is an Aktienbolaget gasaccumulator?
Answer on page 153

GREATER GRAINS

Grains have been the staple diet of human beings for over 10,000 years, yet we are surprisingly conservative about trying new varieties. So if you're bored with pasta and rice, try a few of these:

Buckwheat – this tiny triangular seed is rich in rutin, which strengthens blood vessels, and is a good source of protein

Farro – an ancient grain used by the Greeks, not unlike brown rice but with larger, firmer grains

Freekeh – a traditional middle Eastern grain made from roasted green wheat, with a smokey, nutty taste; high in protein and fibre

Kamut – an ancient Egyptian grain that is high in protein, vitamins and minerals, with a rich, buttery flavour

Maize – gluten-free, so ideal for coeliacs; the grain with which polenta is made

Millet – regarded by many as the most nutritious food in the world; high in protein, low in starch, easily digested, rich in silicon which is good for hair, skin, teeth and nails; and gluten-free

Pearl barley – a small rounded grain like wheat or pudding rice, this ancient Roman grain was the food of gladiators. Contains calcium and potassium and can help to lower cholesterol levels

Quinoa – a tiny, bead-shaped grain, pale gold, easy and quick to cook, with a firm, crunchy texture; rich in protein, amino acids, B vitamins and fibre

Spelt – an ancient grain that is mentioned in the Bible; high in protein with a light and nutty flavour

EXPERT ADVICE

To make perfect pastry, the secret is to keep everything very cold: and that means the ingredients, the utensils and your hands. Use ice water, cold butter and a very cold bowl (metal stays colder than ceramic). Wash your hands in cold water, and repeat if they warm up as you work. Handle the ingredients as little as possible, and leave the pastry to chill and rest in the fridge before you roll it out. It will be as light as a feather.

OLD PICTURE, NEW CAPTION

It is to be noted that in some far-off countries, the natives are still unaware of the invention of cutlery.

QUOTE UNQUOTE

COOKING SAINT

St Martha, who died around 80 AD, was the patron saint of cooking and the sister of the much more famous Mary Magdalene. Martha and Mary lived with their brother Lazarus in Bethany, a small town near Jerusalem. Jesus preached in Judea and often visited their home, and Martha went to great lengths to make Jesus comfortable.

As well as being the patron saint of cooks, she also watches over butlers, dieticians, domestic servants, homemakers, hotel-keepers, housemaids, housewives, innkeepers, laundry workers, maids and servants. In art, Martha is portrayed as a housewife and is often depicted with symbols of housework, such as a broom, ladle or a set of keys. Her feast day is 29th July.

COOKS IN BOOKS

It was through food that I'd first learned to gobble up the world after a childhood as an indifferent eater. To this day, my memories of a transforming student year in Europe... are as dense with the taste of food – my first artichoke, my first celery-root salad with my first remoulade sauce, my first weisswurst and prosciutto – as with images of *pissoirs* along the grand Parisien boulevards, the bombed-out streets of Munich, flamenco dancers on the outskirts of Spanish villages... Other people show snapshots and slides when they come home, but I, returning to New York in 1957, with missionary zeal taught myself to cook in order to make monthly European feasts for friends not lucky enough to have gone abroad in those days when transatlantic travel was prohibitively expensive, when a broiled steak dinner represented the pinnacle of celebration, when Italian food meant spaghetti swimming in tomato sauce. The first person in my family to cross the ocean going east, I felt a calling to introduce my compatriots to such wonders of nature as blood oranges, snails, squash flowers, and fennel. To me food was part of the great postwar cultural adventure: mind-expanding and sensual, titillating and educational, like atonal music or experimental sex, or marijuana, or a new language, only more readily accessible, and I wanted to share the thrill of the flavors of French, German and Italian food that had taken me completely by surprise. As Marco Polo had brought back noodles from China to Italy, so I brought spaghetti alla carbonara from Rome to provincial young New Yorkers.

Alix Kates Shulman, *Drinking the Rain*

BUG EATERS ANONYMOUS

Edible bugs and those who eat them...

Australian aborigines eat witchety grubs, Bogong moths, sugar ants and honeypot ants.

Algerians eat desert locusts, cooked in salt water and dried in the sun before eating.

The Japanese eat hachi-no-ko (boiled wasp larvae), zaza-mushi (aquatic insect larvae), inago (fried ricefield grasshoppers), semi (fried cicada) and sangi (fried silk moth pupae). They also enjoy chocolate-dipped ants.

In Kwara State, Nigeria, West Africa, termites, crickets, grasshoppers, caterpillars, palm weevil larvae, and compost beetle larvae are all delicacies.

Nenet eat lice from their own bodies.

Ethiopians eat honeycomb containing the larvae.

Fried grasshoppers are popular in Africa.

In Asia and Africa, locusts are said to taste like shrimps and are traditionally eaten with honey.

SALAD DAYS

Shakespeare first used the phrase 'salad days' in *Antony and Cleopatra, Act 1, Scene 5*. When Cleopatra lavishes praise on her new love, Antony, one of her attendants reminds the queen that she once felt the same passion for Caesar. Cleopatra replies that she was in her 'salad days, when I was green in judgment: cold in blood'. Cleopatra meant it to mean youthfully naïve, but it has come to mean the best days of one's youth, when life is still full of unexplored potential. It was later the title of a 1950s musical.

CAREFUL WITH THAT FISH BONE

During the most recent year for which figures have been compiled:

- 3,946 people died from an accident in the home.
- 42,000 suffered an accident while eating or drinking.
- 14,000 suffered a non-fatal choking.
- Fish bones were the cause of 4,500 choking accidents.
- The next most common choking culprits were meat or poultry, followed by bones, sweets and coins.
- Under-fives were involved in more choking accidents than any other age group.
- The number of accidents due to choking fell sharply between 1992 and 1993, but is creeping back up.
- Around 41,000 people suffered a poisoning accident.
- Under-fives were involved in more poisoning accidents than any other age group.
- Around 102,000 people burned themselves in the home.
- The key causes of household burns were kettles, steam, hot oil or fat and hot drinks.
- Under-fives were involved in more burn accidents than any other age group.

APRIL FOOD

The poisson d'Avril, the traditional French gift received on 1st April, derives from the 16th century, when Charles IX issued a decree in 1564 that the New Year would henceforth begin on 1st January, instead of 1st April, as it had until then. His people were not amused, and took to sending each other worthless gifts on that day as mock New Year presents. As the sun was in Pisces at the time, the fish shape seemed the obvious choice, and the tradition has survived, so that many French people still give and eat chocolate, marzipan and sugar fish on April Fool's Day.

APPLES AND PEARS

Cockney rhyming slang on a food theme:

almond rocks – socks
apple fritter – bitter (beer)
apples and pears – stairs
bacon and eggs – legs
Bath bun – son
bees and honey – money
biscuits and cheese – knees
bladder of lard – card
bread and butter – gutter
bread and cheese – sneeze
Brussel sprouts – scouts
bubble and squeak – beak (magistrate)
butcher's [hook] – look
carving knife – wife
china plate – mate
chop sticks – six
cocoa – say so
crust of bread – head
currant bun – son
custard and jelly – telly
field of wheat – street
ginger beer – queer
greengages – wages
jam jar – car
kidney punch – lunch
loaf of bread – head
macaroni – pony
mince pies – eyes
old pot and pan – old man
peas in the pot – hot
plates of meat – feet
potatoes in the mould – cold
rabbit and pork – talk
salmon and trout – stout
sausage and mash – cash or crash
tea leaf – thief

QUOTE UNQUOTE

I've had matzo ball soup three meals in a row. Isn't there any other part of the matzo you can eat?
MARILYN MONROE, US actress

Porridge is to the Scots what snow is to the Eskimos – something that needs more than one word to describe it.

blanter – food made from oats
blenshaw – a drink of oatmeal, sugar, milk, water and nutmeg
brochan – thick or thin gruel; sometimes used to mean porridge
brose – a dish of oat or pease-meal mixed with boiling water or milk, with salt and butter added. You can also have **athole brose** (mixed with whisky), **hasty brose** (made quickly), **kail brose** (made with the liquid from boiled kail), **neep brose** (made with the liquid from boiled turnips), **nettle brose** (made with the juice of boiled young nettle-tops) and **water brose** (mixed with boiling water; also known as water broo)
cauld steer(ie) – oatmeal stirred in cold water (or sour milk)
crackins – a dish of fried oatmeal
crannachan, cream crowdie – a dessert of soft fruit, whipped cream and toasted oatmeal
creeshie mealie – fried oatmeal
crowdie, mowdie – oatmeal and water mixed and eaten raw
drammlicks – the small pieces of oatmeal dough which stick to the basin when making oatcakes
drammock – a mixture of raw oatmeal and cold water
forrach – buttermilk, whipped cream or whey with oatmeal stirred in
froh milk – a mixture of cream and whey beaten and sprinkled with oatmeal
girsle – a fragment of crisp or caked porridge
graddan – a coarse oatmeal made from parched grain

grits – oat kernels
gruel – food made of oatmeal
lithocks – a kind of gruel made from fine oatmeal and buttermilk
meal, male – oatmeal
meal an ale – the traditional dish at harvest celebrations, and the celebration itself
meal an thrammel – meal stirred up with water or ale
pap-in – a drink made of light ale and oatmeal, with a little whisky or brandy
parritch, poshie – child's word for porridge
pottage – oatmeal porridge
purry – a savoury dish of oatmeal brose with chopped kail. **Tartan purry** adds chopped red cabbage or boiled cabbage water
skink – a kind of thin, oatmeal and water gruel
skirlie, skirl-in-the-pan – a dish of fried oatmeal and onions
snap and rattle – toasted oatcakes crumbled in milk
sowans – a dish of oat husks and fine meal steeped in water for about a week. After straining, the solid matter at the bottom is the sowans, the liquor is the 'swats' **Deochray** and **grunds** (or grounds) are types of sowans, and **sowan seeds** are the rough husks of oats used in making sowans
sowce – a messy mixture, specifically an oatmeal dish like porridge
stourie, stoorack, stoorin – a kind of liquid fine-oatmeal gruel
wangrace – a kind of thin gruel sweetened with fresh butter and honey and given to invalids

OLD PICTURE, NEW CAPTION

Although Amelia was known for her impeccable manners, she was not to be trusted with a bowl of sticky toffee pudding.

COOKING CONUNDRUMS

Which two fruits are anagrams of each other?
Answer on page 153

GOING UNDERCOVER

The word 'cover', which now refers to a place setting at table, has a slightly murky origin. Until the 15th century, food was served under the cover of a white napkin, which indicated to the diner that all precautions had been taken to avoid the food being maliciously poisoned. Even after this danger subsided, the word stuck and is still routinely used in restaurants. In France during the Ancien Regime, 'cover' was also used to distinguish the king's meals; *au grand couvert* was a large banquet or formal meal, *le petit couvert* was a simple meal that the king ate with intimate friends, although it still consisted of three courses and required 15 attendants to serve it.

Now we have heard how Mrs Sedley had prepared a fine curry for her son, just as he liked it, and in the course of dinner a portion of this dish was offered to Rebecca. 'What is it?' said she, turning an appealing look to Mr Joseph.

'Capital,' said he. His mouth was full of it; his face quite red with the delightful exercise of gobbling. 'Mother, it's as good as my own curries in India.'

'Oh, I must try some, if it is an Indian dish,' said Miss Rebecca. 'I am sure everything must be good that comes from there.'

'Give Miss Sharp some curry, my dear,' said Mr Sedley, laughing.

Rebecca had never tasted the dish before.

'Do you find it as good as everything else from India?' said Mr Sedley.

'Oh, excellent!' said Rebecca, who was suffering tortures with the cayenne pepper.

'Try a chili with it, Miss Sharp,' said Joseph, really interested.

'A chili,' said Rebecca, gasping. 'Oh, yes!' She thought a chili was something cool, as its name imported, and was served with some. 'How fresh and green they look!' she said, and put one into her mouth. It was hotter than the curry; flesh and blood could bear it no longer. She laid down her fork. 'Water, for Heaven's sake, water,' she cried. Mr Sedley burst out laughing (he was a coarse man, from the Stock Exchange, where they love all sorts of practical jokes). 'They are real Indian, I assure you,' said he. 'Sambo, give Miss Sharp some water.'

William Makepeace Thackeray, *Vanity Fair*

CULINARY LEGENDS

Alexis Soyer (1810-1858) was a French cook who fed some of the most important people of his time, but also used his talents to feed the poor. While working in Paris, he rose to become the deputy chef at the Ministry of Foreign Affairs, but after the July revolution of 1830, he moved to England, where he married an English actress. He was appointed head chef at the Reform Club from 1837 to 1850, where he installed the kitchens. These included a gas cooking range, which was unusual for the time, even for a large cooking establishment. In 1847, he was commissioned by the government to open kitchens in Dublin to help feed victims of the Irish famine, and he later served during the Crimean war as a dietary advisor to the British army, improving the rations and inventing more efficient ways to cook in the field. He wrote several books for both wealthy and impoverished gourmets – *The Gastronomic Regenerator* (1846), *The Poor Man's Regenerator* (1848) and *A Shilling Cookery for the People* (1854), the last of which sold a quarter of a million copies.

GILDING THE SAUSAGE

If you see the additive E175 in a list of ingredients, treat that food with respect – the number denotes gold leaf, an authorized additive for charcuterie, confectionery and cake decorations.

EXPERT ADVICE

How to choose the ideal saucepan:

Aluminium
Pros: second most effective heat conductor; lightweight and easy to lift
Cons: easily dented; must be coated with a non-stick surface, as aluminium reacts with certain foods

Cast iron
Pros: Even heat distribution, holds high temperatures well; relatively inexpensive
Cons: Very heavy; must be kept oiled to prevent rusting

Glass
Pros: Good for watching contents of pan; attractive; useful in microwave and oven
Cons: Poor heat conductor; breaks easily

Stainless steel
Pros: Hard, durable; good for keeping food warm and for low-temperature cooking
Cons: Stainless steel is a poor heat conductor, so needs a copper or aluminium base, or aluminium core to increase heat conductivity. If it has these, it is the best option and is much used in the professional kitchen

Copper
Pros: Excellent heat conductor, as it heats and cools rapidly and evenly
Cons: Must be lined with tin, as copper reacts with certain foods, and the tin lining must be replaced periodically; heavy, often expensive; needs frequent cleaning

Enamel
Pros: Conducts heat evenly; hard-wearing
Cons: If poorly made, the enamel can crack, leaving space for bacteria to grow; requires wooden utensils to avoid scratching the enamel

SERVICE NOT INCLUDED

The habit of tipping is said to have begun in the tea gardens of London, where locked wooden boxes were left on the tea tables, and inscribed with the letters T.I.P.S. If customers were impatient for refreshment, they would drop a coin or two in the box as they took their seats 'to insure prompt service'.

ART GOOD ENOUGH TO EAT

The Absinthe Drinker – Manet
Around the Fish – Klee
At the Bar – Toulouse-Lautrec
Belshazzar's Feast – Rembrandt
The Cornfield – Constable
Le Déjeuner sur l'Herbe – Manet
The Dinner Table – Matisse
The Feast of the Rose Garlands – Dürer
Girl Drinking Wine with a Gentleman – Vermeer
The Last Supper – Dali, Holbein the Younger, Leonardo da Vinci
(among many others)
The Luncheon – Manet
The Luncheon of the Boating Party – Renoir
The Milkmaid – Millet
The Milkmaid of Bordeaux – Goya
An Old Woman Cooking Eggs – Velázquez
The Pantry – Hooch
The Potato Eaters – Van Gogh
St Mawes at the Pilchard Season – Turner
The Soup – Picasso
Still Life with Gingerpot – Mondrian
Sunflowers and Pears – Gauguin
The Tête-a-Tête Supper – Toulouse-Lautrec
Tuna Fishing – Dali
Woman with Pears – Picasso
Women with Mangoes – Gauguin

FIRST BEHEAD YOUR SHEEP

To help despairing housewives cope with the task of making palatable meals out of root vegetables, cheap cuts of meat and dried egg, Marguerite Patten published *The Victory Cookbook*, a triumph of optimism over resources. Alongside such recipes as Cabbage Casserole, Beetroot Fricassee and Mock Lemon Curd (cornflour, sugar, margarine and lemon squash) was a tempting recipe called Sheep's Head Roll. To summarise: blanch a sheep's head, tie it in a cloth (to keep the nourishing brains intact), place in pan with vegetables, spices, herbs and vinegar and simmer for one and a half hours. Remove the tongue and thinly slice. Remove the meat from the head, mince it and blend it with the 'softened' vegetables, and some breadcrumbs and flour. Form the meat into a long strip, place the tongue slices down the middle, roll it up and steam for one hour. Allow to cool, then serve cold. The recipe recommends that the cook 'add a little tomato ketchup or Worcestershire sauce to the meat mixture to give additional flavour'.

94 *Increased turnover, in dollars, per square foot in the average US supermarket since 1990*

'Now breakfast,' said Merlyn.

The Wart saw that the most perfect breakfast was laid out neatly for two, on the table before the window. There were peaches. There were also melons, strawberries and cream, rusks, brown trout piping hot, grilled perch which were much nicer, chicken devilled enough to burn one's mouth out, kidneys and mushrooms on toast, fricasee, curry, and a choice of boiling coffee or best chocolate made with cream in large cups.

'Have some mustard,' said Merlyn, when they had got to the kidneys.

The mustard-pot got up and walked over to his plate on thin silver legs that waddled like the owl's. Then it uncurled its handles and one handle lifted its lid with exaggerated courtesy while the other helped him to a generous spoonful.

'Oh, I love the mustard-pot!' cried the Wart. 'Wherever did you get it?'

At this the pot beamed all over its face and began to strut a bit; but Merlyn rapped it on the head with a teaspoon, so that it sat down and shut up at once.

'It's not a bad pot,' he said, grudgingly. 'Only it is inclined to give itself airs.'

TH White, *The Sword in the Stone*

WHO WAS JACK THE TREACLE EATER?

In rural Somerset stands a delightful folly on the edge of the Barwick Estate, marking one of the estate's boundaries. At the edge of a field is a roughly built archway, topped by a crenellated tower entered by an impossibly small door. Perched on the top of the tower is a carefree looking figure: Jack the Treacle Eater. His position is marked on the Ordnance Survey map, but his identity is harder to pinpoint. There are two explanations for his name: first, that Jack was a murderer being sheltered by his wife, who – because she worked in Barwick House kitchens – could smuggle him food, which was mostly treacle. The second is that Jack was employed at Barwick House as a runner to carry messages to London, and was fed on a diet of treacle to give him energy for his task. As London is about 125 miles away, this seems unlikely, and certainly nutritionally unsound. The sugar crash would have kicked in before he got as far as Salisbury.

QUOTE UNQUOTE

I will not eat oysters. I want my food
dead – not sick, not wounded – dead.
WOODY ALLEN, US screenwriter and actor

THE REAL MR BEAN

Henry John Heinz was born in Pittsburgh in 1844 to German immigrant parents and began his retail career by selling jars of horseradish. In 1876, he and his brother John and cousin Frederick set up F&J Heinz. Their first product was ketchup, at the time a homemade staple of every US household, but one that required a whole day of attentive stirring.

The business grew quickly, and by 1886 Henry was in the UK, selling his products to Fortnum and Mason. Heinz opened a company in Britain in 1905, and his beans in tomato ketchup were first made here in 1925, closely followed by the tins of spaghetti, which confused a generation or two about the true consistency of pasta. Heinz fame spread all over the world, and Heinz products were even taken to the South Pole by Scott in 1910, as part of expedition rations. The much-maligned Heinz Salad Cream was invented in the UK in the 1940s to liven up the wartime diet, and became so popular that plans to withdraw it in recent years raised so much protest that it was put back on sale. Today Heinz turns out 1.5 million cans of beans a day, and is the proud owner of one of the most famous advertising slogans of all time: 'Beanz Meanz Heinz'.

QUOTE UNQUOTE

The discovery of a new dish does more for human happiness than the discovery of a new star.
JEAN-ANTHELME BRILLAT-SAVARIN, French lawyer,
magistrate and writer on gastronomy

EXPERT ADVICE

Knives you should have in your cutlery drawer

Boning knife – for removing raw meat from the bone, and for trimming fat
Bread knife – for the obvious use, but can also be used to cut cakes and pastries
Carving knife – for the Sunday roast
Cook's knife – for general chopping, slicing and dicing
Filleting knife – for filleting and skinning fish, and removing membranes from meat
Paring knife – for finer slicing and dicing (also, worryingly, called the 'office knife')

To get the best from your knives, sharpen them regularly; once or twice a month is recommended (restaurant chefs sharpen theirs daily, though their needs are rather different). To test if your knife needs sharpening, try it out on a tomato; a sharp knife will slice through the skin of a tomato with only the slightest of pressure.

FOOD FOR THOUGHT

Ten easy ways in which cooks can help to save the planet

1. Eat more organic foods
To see how this could benefit you (and the farmers and the environment), see www.organicfoods.co.uk.

2. Be a responsible carnivore
When you buy eggs, poultry, fish and meat that are certified organic, you can be sure that the animal has been protected by the highest standards of animal welfare.

3. Support local farmers
Buy direct rather than via a middleman, so local farmers keep more of the profit. See www.farmersmarket.net for your nearest market.

4. Buy seasonal
Buy homegrown fruit and vegetables rather than imported produce.

5. Choose Fairtrade
More of your money gets back to the supplier. See www.fairtrade.org.uk to find out what's on offer.

6. Grow your own
If you have the space, growing your own fruit and vegetables is very satisfying (and if all you have is a windowbox, you can still grow herbs).

7. Conserve heat
Keep oven doors closed and lids on pans to conserve heat when you're cooking.

8. Use the steam
Cook vegetables in the steam from your rice or pasta pan – it saves energy, and steaming conserves vitamins.

9. Make your garden happy
Start a compost heap from kitchen waste, such as uncooked food, fruit, vegetables, teabags and coffee grounds. Add tissues, kitchen towel, toilet roll tubes, egg cartons and cereal boxes. See www.compost.org.uk for how to build your compost heap.

10. Stay dust free
Keep the condenser coils on your fridge free of dust (a dusty coil can increase energy consumption by up to 30%).

WAS HE A GOOD EGG?

Humpty Dumpty was depicted as an egg in Lewis Carroll's Alice books, but the nursery rhyme does not actually say he's an egg, so it is unclear when and why it was first assumed. However, there are many theories about the origin of the nursery rhyme, the most popular of which has been that Humpty represented King Richard III, who fell from his horse in the Battle of Bosworth Field and was hacked to pieces. But the tourist board of East Anglia firmly maintains that Humpty was a powerful cannon used during the Civil War, which was mounted on top of the Wall Church in Colchester to defend the city in the summer of 1648.

WHAT'S THAT SMELL?

Surströmming may be the world's smelliest food. It is a fermented herring popular in Sweden, which was first produced by accident by some dishonest fishermen, who sold their surplus herring stock (which had begun to ferment) to some unsuspecting villagers. When they returned the following year with properly salted herring, the villagers rejected it and asked for the same as the previous year. So the fishermen began to create *surströmming* especially for them.

The herring are placed in a closed barrel with half the usual amount of salt needed to preserve them, and the barrels are left out in the summer sun for some months, then opened to be repacked and sold. The sale causes something of a stampede. In *North Atlantic Seafood*, Alan Davidson records that a fishery official in the area remembered, as a young man, that when the barrels of herring were opened, 'birds began to drop dead from the sky'. The fish is served with chopped red onion, potatoes and, as Davidson relates, 'thin slices of a special bread, *tunnbröd*, which the northerners carry about in their Wellington boots'.

A LAND OF PLENTY

The original meanings of a few British place names:

Accrington – Acorn Farm
Croydon – Saffron Valley
Ely – Eel
Gateshead – Goats Head
Gatwick – Goat Farm
Lundy – Puffin
Purley – Pear-tree Wood
Ramsey – Land of Wild Garlic
Rievaulx – Rye Valley
Stranraer – Fat Peninsula
Swindon – Pig Hill
Tintagel – Throat Fort

LITERARY FEASTS

The typical English sweet, which a friend described to me: 'Cake soaked with bad port, smothered in boiled custard stained a purple brown with blackberry juice, which is in turn top-layered with warm ill-beaten white of egg tinted fuchsia pink, the whole garnished with small dirty-brown buttons of granite that are reported by us hardier Britons to be macaroons. This particular foul concoction is called Queen of Puddings!'

MFK Fisher, *Serve it Forth*

READ, LEARN AND INWARDLY DIGEST

The human digestive system is around 26–33ft long.

The digestive system consists of five parts: mouth, oesophagus, stomach, small intestine and large intestine.

It takes six seconds for liquid and 15 seconds for food to reach the stomach from the mouth.

The epiglottis prevents food from going into your lungs when you eat.

Food is digested in the mouth, stomach and small intestine; the large intestine deals with waste.

The acid in your stomach is hydrochloric.

The human stomach must produce a new layer of mucus every two weeks or it will digest itself.

The stomach capacity is about 2–2.5 pints

It takes from one to five hours for a meal to be digested.

THE TASTE OF GUILT

On 31 December 1995, former French president François Mitterand invited his friends to what he knew would be his last feast, as he was dying from cancer. What surprised his friends was the nature of the meal. Mitterand had decided to go out in style, and despite being extremely ill, ordered a menu of oysters, foie gras, roast capon and, to finish, ortolan. Ornithologists will wince; the ortolan is a very tiny, endangered songbird, barely the size of a big toe, which is illegal to catch and certainly illegal to eat for dinner. Predictably this makes it a much-desired delicacy, and Mitterand decided that he had little to lose by breaking the rules.

The ritual of ortolan-eating dates back to Roman times; the birds are caught, kept in darkness and overfed to increase their size, then drowned in a quantity of Armagnac and roasted for a few minutes. The diner covers his head with an embroidered cloth and puts the bird whole into his mouth, leaving only the head, which he bites off. The bird is then chewed, whole, bones and all, for up to 15 minutes, as the diner savours every last morsel of its newly acquired fat. In a last act of gastronomic defiance, Mitterand ate two. He died a few days later.

QUOTE UNQUOTE

Take away that pudding. It has no theme.
WINSTON CHURCHILL, British politician

One way to become immortal is to have a recipe named after you:

Apple Charlotte – layers of cake crumbs or breadcrumbs and sugar, butter and puréed apple, named after Queen Charlotte, wife of King George III.

Beef Wellington – fillet steak encased in puff pastry named after The Duke of Wellington, prime minister and defeater of Napoleon.

Chateaubriand – a thick cut of beef fillet grilled and served with béarnaise sauce, named after Vicomte de Chateaubriand, French ambassador to London in 1822.

Frangipane – a sweet custard flavoured with almonds and spices, named after Muzio Frangipani. He was a 16th century Italian marquis who created a perfume based on bitter almonds, which Parisian pastry cooks then tried to capture by adding almonds to the custard they used for filling tartlets.

Garibaldi biscuit – a flat, chewy biscuit filled with currants, named after 19th century Italian commander Giuseppe Garibaldi.

Gâteau St Honoré – a pastry circle topped with a ring of choux buns filled with whipped cream, named after St Honorius, the patron saint of pastry cooks.

Madeleine – a miniature sponge cake, traditionally baked in small cockleshell-shaped tins. It is said to be named after Madeleine Palmier, who worked as a pastry cook in France in the 19th century.

Melba toast – bread toasted then split in half to create very thin, crisp toast, and allegedly named by César Ritz when it was served to Dame Nellie Melba, the Australian soprano, at the Ritz in London.

Pavlova – a soft meringue cake topped with fruit and whipped cream, named after Russian ballerina Anna Pavlova and created in her honour during her visit to Australia and New Zealand in the 1920s.

Peach Melba – peaches, ice cream and raspberry sauce, also named after Dame Nellie Melba, and created for her by French master chef Escoffier.

Sally Lunn – a large teacake made with a rich yeast mixture. Tradition has it that Sally was a pastry cook in 18th-century Bath, where she made and sold these buns in the streets.

Sauce Colbert – named after Jean-Baptiste Colbert, Louis XVI's treasurer, Sauce Colbert is a lemon sauce flavoured with parsley and Madeira.

Savarin – a large, ring-shaped, spongy cake made from a rich yeast mixture, soaked in a rum-flavoured syrup and filled with fruit and cream. Named after Jean-Anthelme Brillat-Savarin, historic French gourmet and writer on gastronomy.

Victoria Sandwich – a sponge cake sandwiched together with raspberry jam, named after Queen Victoria.

STRANGE DIETS

Some people like to eat dirt. White kaolin clay has been a foodstuff for certain people for centuries, and is treasured for its flavour with the same enthusiasm that is reserved for truffles. In Mexico, clay tablets replace wafers in an annual religious celebration and some African Americans send packets of clay to expectant mothers. Australian aborigines make a white clay loaf wrapped in leaves and baked; and the Kai people in Papua New Guinea string small balls of clay on a skewer like a kebab and cook them over an open fire. Cheap, delicious and filled with minerals, kaolin clay comes in four varieties: red, white, black and the rarest blue, which contains tiny air bubbles that massage the palate like champagne when eaten.

QUOTE UNQUOTE

To make a good salad is to be a brilliant diplomatist – the problem is entirely the same in both cases. To know exactly how much oil one must put with one's vinegar.
OSCAR WILDE, dramatist and poet

LITERARY FEASTS

Bread became his chief sustenance when his regimen attained to that austerity which afterwards distinguished it. He could have lived on bread alone without repining. When he was walking in London with an acquaintance, he would suddenly run into a baker's shop, purchase a supply, and breaking a loaf, he would offer half of it to his companion. 'Do you know,' he said to me one day, with much surprise, 'that such an one does not like bread? Did you ever know a person who disliked bread?' and he told me that a friend had repulsed such an offer. I explained to him that the individual in question probably had no objection to bread in a moderate quantity, at a proper time and with the usual adjuncts, and was only unwilling to devour two or three pounds of dry bread in the streets, and at an early hour. Shelley had no such scruple; his pockets were generally well-stored with bread. A circle upon the carpet, clearly defined by an ample verge of crumbs, often marked the place where he had long sat at his studies, his face nearly in contact with his book, greedily devouring bread at intervals amidst his profound abstractions. For the most part he took no condiment; sometimes, however, he ate with his bread the common raisins which are used in making puddings, and these he would buy at mean little shops.
Thomas Jefferson Hogg, *The Life of Percy Bysshe Shelley*

A HINT OF NOSTALGIA

When a 2004 supermarket poll identified the UK's favourite smells, not surprisingly the top three were food. Smells can influence our behaviour – a poll conducted in 1996 showed that if a store smelled of lavender, ginger, spearmint and orange, the shoppers rated the shop's merchandise more highly.

Fresh bread...21%
Frying bacon 17%
Coffee..13%
Ironing..11%
Cut grass 8%
Babies 7%
The sea 6%
Christmas trees.. 4%
Perfume 2%
Fish and chips 1%

OUT OF THIS WORLD

When Neil Armstrong and Edwin 'Buzz' Aldrin sat down to eat their first meal on the moon, their lunar meal – served out of foil packs – comprised roast turkey and all the trimmings.

SUFFER THE LITTLE CHILDREN

Pity the Victorian child if its mother believed the dietary advice given in Pye Henry Chavasse's popular treatise on parenthood, *Advice to Mothers on the Management of their Offspring* (1844).

'New potatoes are acceptable, but old potatoes, well-cooked and mealy, are the best a child can have,' he claimed. Chevasse recommended that the under-10s break their fast with warm milk poured over stale bread (at least seven days old), and that they should not be given sweets or green vegetables, as both were little better than poison. The over-10s could drink weak beer and eat a little mutton, but not pork or beef. Conscientious parents took his advice to heart and fed their offspring a grim diet, including gruel made from ground-up biscuits, flour and milk. Chevasse maintained that 'meat, potatoes and bread, with hunger for their sauce, is the best and indeed should be the only dinner they should have'. Modern parents can only conclude that he didn't like children and wanted all the biscuits for himself.

Amount, in milligrammes, of calcium in a 15g portion of sesame seeds

Hannah Glasse (1708-1770) was one of the most popular cookbook writers of her time, which was largely the result of good timing. The Puritans had banned spices and frowned upon rich food, and the end of Puritanism was the beginning of a passion for good food. Hannah's first book, *The Art of Cookery Made Plain and Easy* (1747) was aimed at the inexperienced cook or housewife and not the professional chef. 'I only hope my Book will answer the Ends I intend it for,' wrote Hannah in her introduction, 'which is to improve the Servants, and save the Ladies a great deal of Trouble'. She further believed that 'every servant who can but read will be capable of making a tolerable good Cook'.

Hannah scorned French cookery as fanciful, but cheerfully plagiarised French recipes – copyright was a tenuous idea at the time, and most cookbook writers shamelessly lifted recipes from each other. Samuel Johnson thought that her book must have been written by a man, which was the usual case at the time, 'because women can spin very well, but they cannot make a good book of cookery'. Cookbooks, indeed, were often written by chefs for other chefs, and were hard for ordinary men and women to understand. Glasse presented her recipes plainly and clearly, and assumed that her book would be bought by employers to give to their servants: 'If I have not wrote in the high, polite style, I hope I shall be forgiven; for my intension is to instruct the lower sort, and therefore must treat them in their own way.'

She also wrote the *Servant's Directory* and *The Compleat Confectioner,* published in 1770, the year of her death.

COOKING CONUNDRUMS

You use a knife to slice my head.
You weep beside me when I am dead.
What am I?
Answer on page 153

HOME COMFORTS

When the Duke of Wellington landed at Dover in 1814, after being away from England for six years, the first thing he asked for was an unlimited supply of hot, buttered toast.

FOOD IN THE FIFTIES

The 1950s could be thought of as the culinary era of innocence – the calm before the storm of BSE, GM foods, microwave dinners and Chilean strawberries in January. The men who survived the war had reclaimed their jobs, women went back to the kitchen, and the birth rate soared. When rationing ended in 1954, life began to seem rosy once more. Fresh fruit and vegetables were almost entirely home-grown, so the nation ate seasonally, with the addition of the occasional imported exotic fruit such as bananas and pineapples. Housewives shopped at small specialist shops, buying meat from the butcher, cheese from the grocer and so on. They often shopped daily, as few homes had fridges at the beginning of the decade, and there were more local village shops. Most food was sold loose and was weighed out to order and wrapped in paper. Bread, milk, vegetables and other groceries were delivered to the door. Families spent around one-third of their income on food and drink (by 2001, it was only 16%). However, things were about to change. As well as an end to rationing, the 1950s brought us commercial television; TV's first celebrity chef, Fanny Cradock; Elizabeth David's *Mediterranean Food*; and the first self-service convenience store, opened by J Sainsbury in Croydon.

OLD PICTURE, NEW CAPTION

*While Hubert always enjoyed his birthday celebrations,
he wished that his mother, just once, could have made him
a cake shaped like a train*

FIT THAT IN YOUR SHOPPING TROLLEY

The grocery list for the coronation feast of Pope Clement VI
in May 1344 read as follows:

15 sturgeon
60 pigs
68 barrels of lard and salted meat
80 saumées (each consisting of 500 loaves of bread)
101 calves
118 cows
300 pike
914 kids
1,023 sheep
1,446 geese
1,500 capons
3,043 fowls
7,428 chickens
50,000 tarts (requiring 3,250 eggs)

Also required were 300 jugs, 5,500 pitchers, 2,500 glass flagons,
5,000 glasses and 2,600 drinking bowls. The Pope practised a
little economy with these last items, as they were hired rather
than bought.

LUCKY FOOD

The origin of some foodie superstitions:

Don't spill the salt – this dates back to the days when salt was
expensive, so spilling it was wasteful. Salt is a symbol of friendship
and welcome, and salt and bread is still a traditional gesture of welcome in some cultures.

Do spill your wine – an omen of good luck, as it anticipates celebrations.

Bash in your empty eggshell – eggs were once considered mysterious
and sacred, and it was thought that magicians used them to cast
spells, writing the spell on the inside of the empty eggshell. To crush
the eggshell is to crush the evil spell.

Throw rice at weddings – this wishes the couple prosperity and
abundance in their married life.

Don't cross knives at table – because it symbolises the cross of crucifixion, and the crossing of swords with your enemy.

Don't have 13 people to dinner – because of the association with the
Last Supper. Judas was the 13th man; had he not been there, things
might have turned out quite differently.

Doris discovers the drawbacks to baking double-crust pies.

LITERARY FEASTS

Finally... the *pot-au-feu* itself – the foundation glory of French cooking. Alexandre Dumas the elder wrote in his *Grand Dictionnaire de Cuisine*: 'French cooking, the first of all cuisines, owes its superiority to the excellence of French bouillon.'

...This bouillon is one of the two end products of the pot. The other is the material that has produced it – beef, carrots, parsnips, white turnips, leeks, celery, onions, cloves, garlic, and cracked marrowbones, and, for the dress version, fowl. Served in some of the bouillon, this constitutes the dish known as *pot-au-feu*. Dumas is against poultry 'unless it is old', but advises that 'an old pigeon, a partridge, or a rabbit roasted in advance, a crow in November or December' works wonders. He postulates 'seven hours of sustained simmering', with constant attention to the 'scum' that forms on the surface and to the water level. This supervision demands the full-time presence of the cook in the kitchen throughout the day, and the maintenance of the temperature calls for a considerable outlay in fuel. It is one reason that the pot-au-feu has declined as a chief element of the working-class diet in France. Women go out to work, and gas costs too much.

AJ Liebling, *Between Meals: An Appetite for Paris*

Ideas that changed the way we eat

Canned food: 1795

In the late 18th century, Napoleon promised 12,000 French francs to anyone who could come up with a method of preserving food that could be used by his armies while on campaign. French cook and inventor Nicolas Appert won the prize, though it took him 14 years to perfect his method. Using glass jars sealed with wax and wire, he found that if food is heated and sealed in an airtight container, it will not spoil (although it would be 50 years before Louis Pasteur would explain that it was because the heat in the jar sterilised bacteria). Englishman Peter Durand took the process one step farther in 1810 when he developed a method of sealing food into tin-coated steel containers, the precursor of the modern tin can.

The refrigerator: 1805

The process of artificial refrigeration was first demonstrated by William Cullen at the University of Glasgow in 1748. But it took until 1805 for American inventor, Oliver Evans, to design the first refrigeration machine. The first actual refrigerator was built by Jacob Perkins in 1834.

The egg beater: 1884

African American, Willis Johnson of Cincinnati, Ohio, patented an improved mechanical egg beater on 5 February 1884. His device was more of an early mixing machine than just an egg beater, as

it could mix eggs, batter, and other baker's ingredients, and had two chambers, one of which could be cleaned while the other was beating.

The electric toaster: 1893

The first electric toaster was invented in 1893 in the UK by Crompton and Co and re-invented in 1909 in the US. In July, 1909, Frank Shailor of General Electric submitted his patent application for the D-12, considered the first commercially successful electric toaster. It only toasted one side of the bread at a time and it required a person to stand by and turn it off manually when the toast looked done. Charles Strite invented the modern, pop-up toaster in 1919.

Aluminium foil: 1910

Dr Lauber, Neher & Cie, Emmishofen was opened in Kreuzlingen, Switzerland. The plant was owned by JG Neher & Sons (aluminium manufacturers) and it was Neher's sons together with Dr Lauber who discovered the endless rolling process and the use of aluminium foil as a protective barrier.

The kitchen blender: 1922

Stephen Poplawski invented the blender in 1922, as he was the first person successfully to put a spinning blade at the bottom of a tall container, which proved the winning combination.

The electric kettle: 1922
Arthur Leslie Large invented the electric kettle in 1922, though it had to be switched off manually. General Electric introduced the automatic cut-out in 1930.

The cheese-slicer: 1927
On a hot summer day in Norway in 1927, Thor Bjørklund had his lunch break in his carpenter-workshop at Lillehammer. On discovering four melted slices of cheese, he tried to separate them with his tools; first with his knife, then his saw, and finally with his plane – which worked beautifully. And the rest is cheese history.

The Aga: 1929
Swedish scientist Gustaf Dalén saved thousands of lives with his work on lighthouse technology, for which he won the Nobel Prize for Physics in 1912. His work involved the safe use of acetylene gas, so it is ironic that he was blinded in an experiment involving acetylene cylinders. While recovering at home, Dalén realised how badly designed the kitchen range was. Dalén set about improving its details, and the Aga cooker was launched in 1929. It has proved so popular in the UK that while Sweden stopped has now stopped making Agas, the stoves are still manufactured in Shropshire.

Tupperware: 1947
Tupperware was invented by Earl Silas Tupper, a New Hampshire tree surgeon and plastics innovator, who began experimenting with polyethylene, a new material used primarily for insulation, radar and radio equipment. He patented the Tupperware seal in 1947 and the airtight plastic container proved invaluable to everyone from tea-ladies to Royalty.

The microwave: 1945
Shortly after the end of World War II, US electronics expert Percy Spencer was touring one of his laboratories at the Raytheon Company when he experienced a strange sensation, and noticed that the chocolate bar in his pocket had softened. When he realised he was standing in front of a magnetron, his curiosity was aroused. He held a bag of unpopped corn next to the magnetron and it exploded into puffy white corn. The first microwave oven was sold in 1947, though it was too large for domestic use. The first counter-top microwave went on sale in 1967 for just under US$500.

A ONE-MAN SHOW

Dave Walia set a world record when he prepared and cooked a meal single-handedly for 1,081 guests in 50 hours 30 minutes at Fissul in Portugal in October 1998. Beginning work at 10am on the 22nd, he prepared 2kg of chillies, 10kg of garlic, 10kg of ginger, and 200kg of onions. The next day he made 40 litres of yoghurt, diced 250kg of chicken breasts and on the 24th, he prepared the rice and cooked 2,000 poppadoms.

A NICE JIM SKINNER

Should you find yourself in a Cockney bar or caff, here's how to order your food...

beer – pig's ear
brandy – fine and dandy
bread – Uncle Fred
butter – stammer and stutter
cake – Sexton Blake
cheese – stand at ease
dinner – Jim Skinner
drink – tiddly wink
fish – Lilian Gish
fork – Duke of York
gin – needle and pin
gravy – army and navy
kipper – Jack the Ripper
liver – cheerful giver
pickles – Harvey Nichols
rum – Tom Thumb
scotch – pimple and blotch
soup – loop the loop
steak and kidney – Kate and Sydney
supper – Tommy Tucker
tea – you and me
water – fisherman's daughter
whisky – gay and frisky

And finally...
bill – Jack and Jill (or Beecham's pill)

COOKING CONUNDRUMS

Who had to obtain the apples of Hesperides?
Answer on page 153

ONE POTATO, TWO POTATO

If potato varieties to you means mashed, boiled or baked, read on – England has literally hundreds of varieties of potatoes to taste. And variety, as they say, is the spud of life:

Belle de Fontanay • Charlotte • Desiree • Duke of York
Dundrod • Estima • Fianna • Golden Wonder • Kerr's Pink
Linzer Delikates • Marfona • Lady Balfour • Nadine • Pentland
Javelin • Pink Fir Apple • Premiere • Romano • Saxon • Wilja

MORE FILMS FOR FOODIES

Almonds and Raisins
Animal Crackers
The Apple Dumpling Gang
The Apple Game
Bhaji on the Beach
The Cider House Rules
A Clockwork Orange
Duck Soup
Fried Green Tomatoes
Goodbye Mr Chips
Grease
Like Water For Chocolate
Merci Pour Le Chocolat
Mr Bean
Shooting Fish
Soul Food
A Taste of Honey
There's a Girl in My Soup

FOOD FOR THOUGHT

• To carry the same amount of food, air freight burns 50 litres of fuel, a ship burns one litre, and road transport six litres. As aviation fuel is untaxed, air freight costs about one-quarter of what it costs to transport food by road.

• Distributing food by plane around the world releases 50 times more CO_2 than if it went by sea.

• 1kg of asparagus flown from California produces 4kg of carbon dioxide. If it were grown in Europe, 900 times less energy would be produced.

• The price of sending by sea fell by over 70% between 1980 and 2000.

• In 2001, for every 1,000 fruit products bought in the UK, only six were grown in the UK.

• One tonne of food in the UK now travels an average of 123km (76 miles) before it reaches the shelves, compared with 82km (51 miles) in 1978.

• More than one third of truck traffic on UK roads is carrying food.

• If your Sunday lunch consists of beef from Australia, runner beans from Thailand, potatoes from Italy, carrots from South Africa, broccoli from Guatemala and fruit from America and New Zealand, the ingredients could have travelled a total of 49,000 miles. All of these ingredients are grown in Britain.

110 *Temperature, in degrees fahrenheit, that should not be exceeded when melting chocolate*

THE SECRET TO PERFECT TURKEY

If you are stumped by the annual task of roasting a turkey, Peter Barham, a physicist from Bristol University, claims to have come up with the perfect formula for cooking turkey. He believes that his heat-transfer equation accounts for every relevant variable, including the difference in temperature between fridge and oven.

It also accounts for the ratio of the specific heat of the turkey to the specific heat of the air, and the radius, girth and precise physical geometry of the turkey.

While breast meat benefits from cooking at a high temperature to bring out the flavour, legs and wings are better cooked for longer at lower temperatures. This means that if the cooking time is based on weight, as is traditional, this is likely to result in part of the bird being undercooked and part overcooked or burnt. 'The main problem is that different muscle groups on the breast, wings and legs benefit from different cooking times and temperatures,' said Dr Barham.

The scientist says his formula shows how to calculate the complete temperature profile of the turkey at all times, but as the formula is hard for a domestic cook to apply, it may be best simply to take note of his conclusion: 'The best method is to split the bird into separate pieces and cook the breast, legs and wings separately.'

However, if you must cook the bird whole, Dr Barham suggests that you cover the breast with aluminium foil to keep the legs and wings cooler than the rest of the bird, but still heated to a sufficient temperature.

COOKS IN BOOKS

Gas and electricity have killed the magic of fire, but in the country many women still know the joy of kindling live flames from inert wood. With her fire going, woman becomes a sorceress; by a simple move-ment, as in beating eggs, or through the magic of fire, she effects the transmutation of substances: matter becomes food. There is enchant-ment in these alchemies, there is poetry in making preserves; the house-wife has caught duration in the snare of sugar, she has enclosed life in jars. Cooking is revelation and creation; and a woman can find special satisfaction in a successful cake or a flaky pastry, for not everyone can do it: one must have the gift.

Simone de Beauvoir, *The Second Sex*

COOKING REVOLUTIONS

In *Food: A History,* Felipe Fernández-Armesto identified eight revolutions in the history of cooking and eating:

The invention of cooking
This set humankind on a course apart from other species towards civilization. Raw food means nature, cooked means culture. Cooking increased the number of foods we could eat, and often improved the nutritional content.

The ritualisation of eating
All societies develop rituals, superstitions and taboos concerning food, which create social bonds and divisions and give food a greater significance than mere nourishment.

The invention of herding
Herding animals instead of hunting them allowed people to settle in one place rather than continuously follow their key food source. Energy spent on hunting could be diverted into other pursuits – such as building settlements, social interaction and leisure pursuits.

The invention of agriculture
Herding and agriculture are ranked by Fernández-Armesto as two of the greatest revolutions of all. The farming of plants did more, in the long run to alter the world than any previous human innovation. Plants are 90% of the world's food, and almost all the animals in the human food chain are fed by fodder grown by farmers.

The rise of inequality
As people separated themselves into groups, food became a social differentiator, indicating class and rank. In many of the earliest civilisations, food was used as means to measure social status. It also led to the development of *haute cuisine* – cooking to satisfy more than simple hunger.

The long range trade in food
The trading of foodstuffs, from spices to sugar, was an exchange of culture as well as food. It internationalised food and established political connections, trading relationships and allies. It opened up the world.

The ecological exchanges
As countries discovered new foods, they began to grow them themselves. Food was not just traded in its finished state, but taken from its source and grown abroad.

The industrialisation and globalization of food
New methods of food production and the growth of industry in general in the 19th and 20th centuries meant that man could produce more food, and faster, growing not just greater quantities, but more varieties of food. This changed both our diet and trading balances across the world.

COOKING SAINT

Macarius the Younger, also known sometimes as Macarius of Alexandria, is the patron saint of confectioners, cooks and pastry chefs. He was born in the early 4th century in Alexandria, Egypt and was a successful merchant in fruits, sweets and pastries. However, when he converted to Christianity, he gave up his business in 335 AD to be a monk in the Thebaid, Upper Egypt. After several years, he travelled to Lower Egypt, was ordained, and lived in a desert cell with other monks, practising severe austerities. For seven years – perhaps to erase the indulgences of his original profession – he lived on raw vegetables dipped in water with a few crumbs of bread, moistened with drops of oil on feast days. He submitted himself to a number of deprivations and trials, including 20 days and 20 nights in the desert without sleep, burnt by the sun in the day and frozen by bitter cold at night; and six months living naked in the marshes, beset by vicious blood-sucking flies and mosquitoes. The experience left him so deformed that when he returned to the monks, they could recognise him only by his voice. He died around 401 AD.

WE WOULD LIKE TO THANK…

A few small culinary inventions that changed the way we eat – though not all of them for the better…

Invention	By	Date
Solid chocolate	Francois-Louis Cailler	1819
Doughnut with hole	Hanson Gregory	1847
Chewing-gum	John Curtis	1848
Potato crisps	George Crum	1853
Condensed milk	Gail Borden	1856
Margarine	Hippolyte Mège-Mouries	1869
Vending machine	Percival Everitt	1883
Coca-Cola	Dr John Pemberton	1886
Vacuum flask	James Dewar	1892
Ready-to-eat breakfast cereal (Shredded Wheat)	Henry D Perky	1893
Ice cream cones	Italo Marcioni	1896
Instant coffee	Nestlé	1937
Food processor	Kenneth Wood	1947
Non-stick pan	Marc Gregoir	1954

QUOTE UNQUOTE

The rich would have to eat money if the poor did not provide food.
RUSSIAN PROVERB

FROM THE COOK'S MOUTH

Although it's possible to love eating without being able to cook, I don't believe you can ever really cook unless you love eating. Such love, of course, is not something which can be taught, but it can be conveyed – and maybe that's the point.

…The French, who've lost something of their culinary confidence in recent years, remain solid on this front. Some years ago in France, in response to gastronomic apathy and consequent lowering of standards nationally, Jack Lang, then Minister of Culture, initiated *la semaine du goût*. He set up a body expressly to go into schools and other institutions not to teach anyone how to cook, but how to eat. This group might take with it a perfect baguette, an exquisite cheese, some local speciality cooked *comme il faut*, some fruit and vegetables grown properly and picked when ripe, in the belief that if the pupils, if people generally, tasted what was good, what was right, they would respect these traditions; by eating good food, they would want to cook it. And so the cycle continues.

Nigella Lawson, *How to Eat*

ORGANIC WORLD

Who buys the most organic food?

Country	GB£ per head in 2000
Denmark	61.34
Switzerland	51.46
Austria	26.41
Sweden	24.25
Netherlands	20.57
Germany	16.42
USA	14.09
France	11.45
Japan	10.64
New Zealand	8.32
UK	8.26
Australia	4.91

QUOTE UNQUOTE

We may live without poetry, music and art;
We may live without conscience, and live without heart;
We may live without friends; we may live without books;
But civilized man cannot live without cooks.
OWEN MEREDITH, poet

AND IT ALL TASTES LIKE CHICKEN

Zoophagy, the practice of eating exotic species of animal for pleasure, was perhaps most memorably practised by Francis Trevelyan Buckland (1826-88). In *Rogues, Villains and Eccentrics*, William Donaldson records that Buckland, a keen amateur naturalist, kept a small menagerie while studying at Oxford University, including a chameleon, an eagle, a jackal, some marmots and a bear named after the king of Assyria. As a small boy he had cooked up squirrel pie and battered mice, but his tastes in adulthood grew more extravagant, stretching, for example, to a panther, which he had sent over from the Surrey Zoological Gardens. Over the years he tried whale, elephant trunk ('rubbery'), rhinoceros pie, porpoise, and a giraffe that had been pre-cooked, thanks to a fire in the giraffe house. A high point in his gastronomic career was perhaps the Eland Dinner, held at the London Tavern in 1859, at which he attempted to persuade his fellow diners that eland should become part of the national diet. We must assume he was not successful, but the assembled company nevertheless enjoyed a menu of sea slug, deer soup and kangaroo.

COOKING CONUNDRUMS

A man was walking down a road carrying a basket of eggs. As he walked he met someone who buys one-half of his eggs plus one-half of an egg. A little further he meets another person who buys one-half of his eggs plus one-half of an egg. Later he meets another person who buys one-half of his eggs plus one half an egg. At this point he has sold all of his eggs, and he never broke an egg. How many eggs did the man have to start with?

Answer on page 153

I'D LIKE TO TEACH THE WORLD TO DRINK

In 2002, the most valuable product in the world was Coca-Cola, outstripping even Microsoft by having a brand value of $69,637,000,000. (McDonald's trailed in at number eight with a value of $26,375,000,000.) Coca-Cola was also the most advertised food or drink in the UK, as the company spent £16,497,785 on promoting their product. The next three brands on this advertising spend list were Guinness, Budweiser and Carling. The first food on the list, in at number four, was the KitKat bar.

After the third fly-in-the-soup joke that day, Harold finally lost his sense of humour.

A GOOD GRILLING

The word barbecue probably comes from *barbacoa*, a Haitian word meaning grill, although another theory suggests that it arose from the French phrase *de la barbe á la queue* (from beard to tail), referring to a whole animal being roasted. The barbecue and its many outdoor derivatives, from the Hawaiian luau to the Japanese hibachi grill, are popular the world over, possibly because we love its simple, barbarian nature, and because a whole roasted animal was for so long a central part of any celebratory feast. Indeed, most people in the UK (84%) choose to use charcoal on their barbecue rather than gas, which is much simpler and more reliable, but takes away all the fun of building a fire. In the UK, barbecuing is a major leisure activity: nearly 50% of households own a barbecue grill of some kind, and it was estimated that in 2003, we held a total of around 54 million barbecues.

FAVOURITE SOUPS

Alexander II
(1855–1881, Russian tsar)
Borscht; which he would only eat on Saxony porcelain

Madame du Barry
(1743–1793, Louis XV's mistress)
Cauliflower soup: she and the King refused anything else as a starter

Sarah Bernhardt
(1844–1923)
Bouillabaisse, which had to be stirred with a red-hot poker

Napoleon Bonaparte
(1769–1821)
Chestnut soup; a comfort soup after recovering from a stomach ache in Egypt

Eva Braun
(1910–1945, Hitler's mistress and, very briefly, wife)
Turtle soup

Al Capone
(1899–1947)
Minestrone – except in 1923 when arch rivals, the Aiellos, offered the chef at Joe Esposito's Bella Napoli Cafe US$35,000 (GB£18,900) if he'd lace the soup with prussic acid. The chef accepted then thought better of it and told his good customer about the plot.

Catherine the Great
(1762–1796)
Borscht, which she ate from handmade silver plates given to her by Ukrainian Cossacks

Charles Darwin
(1809–1882)
Young tortoise soup, which he described as an 'excellent soup'

from his days in the Galapagos Islands

Charles de Gaulle
(1890–1970)
Toutes les soupes – so much so that he insisted on a different one each day

Valery Giscard D'Estaing
(1926–)
'VGE' soup; a truffle soup under a puff pastry lid created in his honour by chef Paul Bocuse

Alexandre Dumas
(1802–1870)
Cabbage soup from his own *Grand Dictionnaire de Cuisine*

Erik XIV
(16th-century Swedish King)
Yellow pea soup – at least until 1577 when he died after eating a poisoned bowlful

Frederick the Great
(1712–1786)
Beer soup – for breakfast at any rate: he proclaimed against coffee in 1777, reasoning that if beer soup was good enough for him, it was good enough for the common folk. Apart from beer, the soup is made of sugar, egg yolks, and cream, seasoned and sprinkled with cinnamon.

James A Garfield
(1831–1881, US President)
Squirrel soup

Adolf Hitler
(1889–1945)
Vegetable soup – Hitler became a vegetarian late in life, and chose to dine primarily on soup, eggs, and vegetables. He particularly liked the vegetable soup cooked

for him by 24-year-old Marlene von Exner, although she later admitted that she secretly added marrowbone.

Howard Hughes
(1905–1976)
Tinned soup, which was all he ate after withdrawing from the world

Vladimir Lenin
(1870–1924)
Shchi (a humble cabbage soup he prepared himself)

Abraham Lincoln
(1809–1865, US President)
Mock turtle soup – the soup he ordered on the 4th March 1861 at a luncheon to celebrate his inauguration as President

Louis XIV
(1638–1715)
Spiced broth – he was known to eat four bowls at both lunch and dinner.

Richard Nixon
(1913–94)
Nixon didn't like soup. After his first state dinner as President, he complained that the meal had gone on too long and that the soup course should henceforth be omitted. 'Men don't really like soup,' he explained.

Rudolf Nureyev
(1938–1992)
Borscht – according to *The Ballet Cookbook*, 1966, Nureyev liked his food to be 'a soup using half a cow'.

Madame de Pompadour
(1721–1764, mistress to King Louis XIV)
Celery soup, which she thought would remedy her sexual frigidity

Franklin Delano Roosevelt
(1882–1945)
Martha Washington's crab soup; served with a splash of Harvey's Bristol Cream Sherry

Frank Sinatra
(1915–1998)
Campbell's Chicken and Rice Soup, which he demanded be served before concerts

Queen Victoria
(1819–1901)
Chicken and ham soup with cream, mushrooms and tapioca

Boris Yeltsin
(1931–)
Fish soup, the recipe for which was included in his autobiographical *Midnight Diaries*. At a working dinner in 1995 with then Prime Minister John Major Yeltsin pushed away his plate of shrimp to complain: 'The prime minister has soup and I don't.' He was swiftly served soup, unaware that Major had requested an alternative because shellfish do not agree with him.

FEEDING THE IMAGINATION

On emerging from one of his creative binges, during which he reportedly lived on too much coffee, eggs and fruit, Honoré de Balzac, author of *La Comédie Humaine,* embarked on a long feast during which he ate 100 Ostend oysters, 12 cutlets of salt-meadow mutton, a duck with turnips, two partridges and a Normandy sole, as well as desserts, fruit, coffee and liqueurs.

MORE FILMS FOR FOODIES

Alice's Restaurant
An Angel at My Table
Babette's Feast
Breakfast at Tiffany's
The Cars that Ate Paris
Delicatessen
Eat the Rich
Festen
Guess Who's Coming to Dinner
My Dinner with Andre
Picnic at Hanging Rock
The Spitfire Grill
Stay Hungry
The Wedding Banquet

THE REAL CAPTAIN BIRDSEYE

Clarence Birdseye (1886–1956) was the creator of the modern frozen food industry.

During World War I, Birdseye lived in Labrador with his wife, where he observed the people of the Arctic preserving fresh fish and meat in barrels of sea water; which were quickly frozen by the arctic temperatures, Clarence Birdseye concluded that it was the rapidity of the freezing that made food retain its freshness when thawed and cooked months later. In 1923, with an investment of $7 for an electric fan, buckets of brine and cakes of ice, Clarence Birdseye invented a system of packing fresh food into waxed cardboard boxes and flash-freezing it under high pressure.

The Goldman-Sachs Trading Corporation and the Postum Company (later the General Foods Corporation) bought Clarence Birdseye's patents and trade marks in 1929 for $22 million. The first quick-frozen vegetables, fruits, seafoods, and meat were sold to the public for the first time in 1930 in Springfield, Massachusetts, under the tradename Birds Eye Frosted Foods. The first individual frozen meal – chicken fricassee and steak – was sold in 1939.

WORLD'S MOST EXPENSIVE COOKBOOK

Cuoco Secreto di Papa Pio Quinto ('The Private Cook of Pope Pius V') by Bartolomeo Scappi was first published in 1570. A surviving 1596 edition was offered for sale by bookseller Martayan Lan in New York, priced US$11,500.

Sometimes it is the only worthwhile product you can salvage from a day: what you make to eat... Cooking therefore, can keep a person who tries sane.
JOHN IRVING, US writer

LITERARY FEASTS

For other breakfast things, George suggested eggs and bacon, which were easy to cook, cold meat, tea, bread and butter, and jam. For lunch, he said, we could have biscuits, cold meat, bread and butter, and jam – but no cheese. Cheese, like oil, makes too much of itself. It wants the whole boat to itself. It goes through the hamper, and gives a cheesy flavour to everything else there. You can't tell whether you are eating apple-pie or German sausage, or strawberries and cream. It all seems cheese. There is too much odour about cheese.

'We shan't want any tea,' said George (Harris's face fell at this); 'but we'll have a good round, square, slap-up meal at seven – dinner, tea, and supper combined.'

Harris grew more cheerful. George suggested meat and fruit pies, cold meat, tomatoes, fruit, and green stuff. For drink, we took some wonderful sticky concoction of Harris's, which you mixed with water and called lemonade, plenty of tea, and a bottle of whisky, in case, as George said, we got upset.

It seemed to me that George harped too much on the getting-upset idea. It seemed to me the wrong spirit to go about the trip in.

But I'm glad we took the whisky.

Jerome K Jerome, *Three Men in a Boat*

FOOD FOR THOUGHT

- In the UK in 1980, 8% of men and 6% of women were obese. By 1995 this had risen to 16% of men and 18% of women. By 2001, the figures were 21% of men and 23% of women.

- In 1990, 5% of six to 15-year-olds were obese. In 2001, 16% of six to 15-year-olds were obese. In 1998, 9% of preschool children were obese.

- If obesity in the UK continues to increase at its current rate, by 2020 one-third of all adults, one-fifth of boys and one-third of girls will be obese.

- Obesity causes about 30,000 deaths in the UK, through related conditions such as heart disease, stroke and diabetes. We spend £500 million a year treating obesity and its related problems.

120 *Cost, in millions of pounds, of removing pesticides from the UK water supply each year*

FIRST 10 THINGS YOU LEARN AT LEITH'S

The Leith School of Cookery in London is one of the UK's top culinary training schools. Here are the first 10 things they teach their aspiring cooks:

1. Knife skills – how to finely dice an onion and reduce a carrot to batons
2. How to write a cook's timeplan (what to do in what order and how long it takes)
3. Emulsions – eg how to make mayonnaise
4. Seasoning – how to season correctly, starting with vegetable soup
5. Eggs – the perfect omelette
6. Pastry – the secrets of shortcrust
7. Custard – how to make crème anglaise
8. The importance of presentation (demonstrated by making a fruit salad)
9. Stock – making clear chicken stock
10. How and why to brown meat

FAMOUS GLUTTONS

Maximinus the Thracian was said to be able to drink an amphora of wine and consume 40 to 60lbs of meat at a single sitting.

Clodius Albinus, an esteemed Roman Emperor, could eat 500 figs, a basket of peaches, 10 melons, 20lbs of grapes, 100 warblers and 400 oysters in one meal.

Vitellius, another Roman Emperor, had a favourite dish that consisted of pike liver, pheasant brains, peacock brains, flamingo tongues and lamprey roe, scarce ingredients that had to be gathered from all corners of his Empire. He 'thought nothing of snatching lumps of meat or cake off the altar, almost out of the sacred fire, and bolting them down.'

Philoxenos, a great epicure, was said by Aristotle to wish he had a longer neck, to enjoy the food for longer.

Louis XIV ate so much at his wedding feast that he was incapacitated.

Duke Ellington, jazz musician, claimed to enjoy eating until it hurt.

Monsieur Creosote exploded at the end of the restaurant scene in Monty Python's *The Meaning of Life*. The wafer-thin mint that proved fatal has since become a British catchphrase.

Elvis Presley in his later years consumed too much of everything, and died of heart failure aged 42. One of his favourite meals – which he would eat as a midnight snack – consisted of a whole loaf of bread filled with peanut butter, jam and bacon.

At last the Red Queen began. 'You've missed the soup and the fish,' she said. 'Put on the joint!' And the waiters set a leg of mutton before Alice, who looked at it rather anxiously, as she had never had to carve one before.

'You look a little shy; let me introduce you to that leg of mutton,' said the Red Queen. 'Alice – Mutton; Mutton, Alice.' The leg of mutton got up in the dish and made a little bow to Alice; and she returned the bow, not knowing whether to be frightened or amused.

'May I give you a slice?' she said, taking up the knife and fork, and looking from one Queen to the other.

'Certainly not,' the Red Queen said, very decidedly: 'it isn't etiquette to cut anyone you've been introduced to. Remove the joint!' And the waiters carried it off, and brought a large plum-pudding in its place.

'I won't be introduced to the pudding, please,' Alice said rather hastily, 'or we shall get no dinner at all. May I give you some?'

But the Red Queen looked sulky, and growled 'Pudding – Alice; Alice – Pudding. Remove the pudding!' and the waiters took it away before Alice could return its bow.

However, she didn't see why the Red Queen should be the only one to give orders, so, as an experiment, she called out 'Waiter! Bring back the pudding!' and there it was again in a moment like a conjuring trick. It was so large that she couldn't help feeling a little shy with it, as she had been with the mutton; however, she conquered her shyness by a great effort, and handed a slice to the Red Queen.

'What impertinence!' said the Pudding. 'I wonder how you'd like it, if I were to cut a slice out of you, you creature!'

Alice could only look at it and gasp.

'Make a remark,' said the Red Queen: 'it's ridiculous to leave all the conversation to the pudding!'

Lewis Carroll, *Through the Looking-Glass and What Alice Found There*

EXTREME EATING

David Hirschkop may have developed the world's most dangerous food – Dave's Insanity Sauce. His homemade chilli sauce is so explosively potent that he uses only one drop in any given recipe, and even at that concentration it was enough to get him banned from the annual National Fiery Food Show in Albuquerque after one taster suffered a mild heart attack. For fans of *The Simpsons*, it was the inspiration for the Guatemalan Insanity Sauce that gave Homer Simpson a funny turn in one memorable episode in 1997.

GIVE US OUR DAILY... MILK

Average weekly consumption of food per person in the UK in 2002:

Milk and cream..2,140g
Meat/meat products 966g
Flour and other cereals (excl bread) 788g
Fresh fruit..745g
Fresh veg (excl potatoes)..732g
Bread..720g
Fresh potatoes 707g
Processed vegetables (inc potatoes).................................546g
Processed fruit and nuts 375g
Fats..186g

COOKING CONUNDRUMS

In a marble hall white as milk
Lined with skin as soft as silk
Within a fountain crystal-clear
A golden apple doth appear.
No doors there are to this stronghold,
Yet thieves break in to steal its gold.
What is it?
Answer on page 153

A STRANGE LOVE OF CUSTARD

Director Stanley Kubrick always intended his film *Dr Strangelove*, released in 1964, to end in a huge custard pie fight between the Russians and the Americans in the War Room (which is why you can see a huge table of food in the final version). The footage was shot, but Kubrick decided that it was too farcical to fit in with the rest of the film. Another reason was that, as President Muffley took a pie in the face, he fell down, and General Turgidson cried 'Gentlemen! Our gallant young president has just been struck down in his prime!' The scene was cut, because of sensitivity over the assassination of JFK.

QUOTE UNQUOTE

*It would be nice if the Food and Drug Administration stopped
issuing warnings about toxic substances and just gave me the names
of one or two things still safe to eat.*
ROBERT FUOSS, US journalist

WEBSITES FOR A BETTER DIET

www.bareingredients.co.uk
A guide to what's in season in the northern and southern hemisphere, plus articles on healthy eating.

www.bigbarn.co.uk
Search for local producers and read lots of information on healthy eating, food campaigns and other food news, plus food facts about what's good for you. Its key aim is to connect local producers with customers, but it is a great source of other information.

www.fairtrade.org.uk
Remind yourself which coffee, chocolate, marmalade and other foods help to support farmers across the world.

www.finefoodworld.co.uk
Where to find fine food awards and fine food suppliers.

www.foodcomm.org.uk
The campaign for food safety in the UK.

www.foodlink.org.uk
Useful advice on food safety for conscientious cooks.

www.foodloversbritain.com
The website for fresh foodies, as it champions the UK farmer, the small producer and the buyer of good quality food. Seasonal foods are highlighted with recipes to match, and you can search for local producers.

www.foodstandards.gov.uk
Lots of facts and figures on nutrition, food safety, healthy eating and seasonal foods Less earnest than it sounds, this is packed with information and even has a few jokes...

www.nutrition.org
Nutritional facts and figures

www.nutritiouslygourmet.com
Up-to-date nutrition news

www.soilassociation.org
The website of the Soil Association, the champion of organic foods.

www.slowfood.com
The website of an organisation devoted to the proper appreciation of good food in the face of an onslaught of its enemy: (boo, hiss) fast food.

www.thecarf.co.uk
The website for the Campaign for Real Food; help in finding good local food, advice on what's in season (including a list to stick on the fridge), online magazine and lots of useful links to like-minded organisations.

DORMOUSE PIE

Lewis Carroll may have been on to something when he put his fictional dormouse in a teapot. This small rodent was a delicacy in Roman times, and the Romans fattened them up by keeping them in small dried mud containers, and feeding them acorns and chestnuts through a small hole. When deemed plump enough, they were stewed or roasted and coated with honey and seeds. Dormouse pie continued to be enjoyed in France until the 17th century.

VENICE TREACLE

Venice treacle was a remedy against poison, developed in Italy, and used across Europe until the 19th century. Also known as theriac, it was an ancient remedy consisting of up to 70 drugs, pounded and mixed with honey. Treacle has been used as an antidote to poison since ancient times; the word treacle is thought to mean 'antidote to the bite of a wild beast'. The recipe for Venice treacle spread all over the world and can be found in the historical medical records of most countries. It is even mentioned in Daniel Defoe's *Journal of the Plague Year*: 'Others think that Venice treacle is sufficient of itself to resist the contagion... I several times took Venice treacle, and a sound sweat upon it, and I thought myself well fortified against the infection.'

A FOODIE STORY

Thinking up a title for your memoirs is never easy, but these celebrities had their minds on food at the time...

Apple Sauce	Michael Wilding
Arias and Raspberries	Harry Secombe
Change Lobsters and Dance	Lili Palmer
Cider with Rosie	Laurie Lee
Confessions of an English Opium-Eater	Thomas de Quincey
Diet for Life	Lynn Redgrave
The Good, The Bad and The Bubbly	George Best
Grain of Wheat	Lord Longford
Let the Chips Fall	Rudy Vallee
Life is a Banquet	Rosalind Russell
The Long Banana Skin	Michael Bentine
Toast: The Story of a Boy's Hunger	Nigel Slater

WORTH HIS SALT

You might think that salt would be the cheapest and simplest thing on the table, but not so. The varying taste and texture of different salts is a hotly debated topic among gastronomes, and the world's finest salt is currently deemed to be Oshima Island Blue Label Salt. It comes from the highly salted waters around this remote Japanese island and can be bought only by members of the very exclusive Blue Salt Club, of which US food critic and culinary detective Jeffrey Steingarten claims to be the only American member. The salt, not surprisingly, is very expensive. Steingarten admits in his book *It Must've Been Something I Ate*: 'I use it infrequently, so as not to squander it all before next year's harvest. In fact, I don't use it at all. How chic is that?'

Machine for the electric extraction of poisons.
Patented 5 July 1898

FOOD FOR THOUGHT

A few things you may find in store-bought food...

Colourings – used to modify the colour of a product

Preservatives – added to food to prevent the growth of harmful micro-organisms, and so allow food to last longer while being transported. Include sulphur dioxide, sulphites, sodium nitrate, sodium nitrite, potassium nitrate, potassium nitrite

Antioxidants – added to food to stop oils and fats from going rancid

Anti-caking agents – used to stop the absorption of water and to prevent powdered mixtures sticking together

Emulsifiers and stabilisers – used to make sure that water and oil stay mixed together

Thickeners – used to thicken a product

Flavour enhancers – chemicals to improve the flavour of the food. There are 36 compounds of flavour enhancer with the most commonly known one being monosodium glutamate (MSG)

QUOTE UNQUOTE

Never serve oysters in a month that has no paycheck in it.
PJ O'ROURKE, US humorist and political commentator

THE WAY WE WERE

From the household accounts of Lord William Howard's steward at
Naworth Castle in Cumberland (c.1619):

Bought of Mr Hall at St Luke's fair by my wyfe:

A quarter of c of reysons solis [sun raisins]..........................xvi s iii d
c of fine currants ....lii s
140 li of powder suger, at 13d ....vii li xi s viii d
One pound of mace and cloves..1/2 li xii s
ii li of licorace ....xii d
One l of anyseeds..x d
ii li of large cynomom ....vii s iiii d
x li of jurden [Jordan] almonds, at 16d ....xiii s iiii d
12 li of case pepper at 2s 4d..xxxviii s
One loafe of suger of xiii li, xi ounces ....xvii s ii d
viii li of large ginger...viii s
One pound of a case of nutmegs...iiii s
One gallon of olives...viii s
6 li of cappers [capers]...viii s
2 li d. of wett sucket [sweets]...iii s ix d
One pound of candied ginger...iiii s
2 barrells for olives and sucketts ....ix d
saffron...xii d
Nutmeggs...xxii d
Sanders [Indian wood for dyeing jellies] ....vi d

c = hundredweight; l and li = pounds (*liber* and *libri*);
s = shillings; d = pence

STRANGE DIETS

A 78-year-old Chinese woman was reported in the *South China
Morning Post* in 2003 to have eaten around 10 tonnes of soil over
the past 70 years. Hao Fenglan from Zhangwu county in northern
China began eating mud and dirt at the age of eight, and claimed to
feel physical discomfort if she did not eat dirt at least once a day.
The newspaper reported that the diet seemed to have done her little
harm, as she appeared to be in good health.

STORM IN A TEACUP

The Boston Tea Party is history's great misnomer; it was fuelled by anger, started a war and there were no fairy cakes involved. By 1773 Britain repealed all 'unfair' taxes on goods imported by America apart from the one on tea, which they kept, largely to make the point that they had the right to impose such taxes on their colonies. In protest, some American ports began to turn away tea deliveries from Britain. In retaliation, the British East India Company began to export tea to the US at so low a price they thought it would be bound to sell. Instead, the Americans rebelled. In December 1773, a group of American radicals dressed as Mohawk Indians boarded a vessel in Boston Harbour and threw its cargo of tea, worth around £18,000 at the time, overboard. Britain ordered the port closed until the cost was repaid. Their intransigence led to the meeting of the First Continental Congress (all of the American colonies bar Georgia) in 1774, which banned all imports from and exports to Britain. Then in 1776, America declared its independence from Britain, and the American War of Independence began.

COOKS IN BOOKS

If you wish to grow thinner, diminish your dinner,
And take to light claret instead of pale ale;
Look down with an utter contempt upon butter,
And never touch bread till it's toasted – or stale.

Henry S Leigh, *A Day for Wishing*

DOLING OUT THE RATIONS

An early form of income support was practised in Rome around 70 BC, but used food rather than money. The cost of living had risen so much that free grain was given away to the needy, about 40,000 people. The numbers rose rapidly; some years later Julius Caesar, concerned that the situation was getting out of hand, was forced to cut the number of people receiving free rations to 150,000. However the numbers went back up again and within 50 years, 320,000 people were receiving the grain – about a third of the population. Three centuries later, the problem was still not solved; the *annona* or handout consisted of bread, pork fat and wine. As the days of the Roman empire drew to a close, however, government officials were finally forced to put an end to free food distribution. The people were left to fend for themselves.

WHAT AM I WAITING FOR?

There is nothing quite like the joy of waiting, cutlery poised, for the first new potatoes, the first strawberries and the first crisp russets of the year to appear. Here is a guide to some seasonal, homegrown delights:

January
Beetroot, brussels sprouts, cabbage, carrots, cauliflower, celeriac, curly kale, Jerusalem artichokes, leeks, parsnips, Swiss chard
Grapefruit, forced rhubarb, Seville oranges

February
Beetroot, broccoli, carrots, curly kale, Jerusalem artichokes, leeks, parsnips, purple sprouting broccoli, Savoy cabbage, spinach, Swiss chard
Blood oranges, forced rhubarb, pink grapefruit, Seville oranges

March
Broccoli, spring greens, spinach, spring onions, kale, leeks
Rhubarb

April
Broccoli, spring greens, spinach, spring onions, kale, leeks
Rhubarb

May
Asparagus, baby carrots, broad beans, broccoli, early cucumbers, new potatoes, lettuce, mangetout, peas
Cherries, rhubarb

June
Asparagus, baby carrots, broad beans, broccoli, cauliflower, courgettes, cucumbers, fennel, garlic, globe artichokes, lettuce, mangetout, new potatoes, peas, rocket, radishes, samphire, spring onions, turnips, watercress
Cherries, gooseberries, rhubarb, strawberries

July
Bok choy, broccoli, carrots, cauliflower, chillies, courgettes, cucumbers, fennel, French beans, garlic, globe artichokes, lettuce, new potatoes, radishes, rocket, runner beans, tomatoes, turnips
Apricots, blackcurrants, blueberries, cherries, gooseberries, loganberries, mulberries, nectarines, passion fruit, peaches, raspberries, redcurrants, strawberries, tayberries, whitecurrants

August and September
Aubergines, beetroot, bok choy, broccoli, carrots, cauliflower, celeriac, chillies, courgettes, cucumbers, fennel, French beans, garlic, globe artichokes, kohlrabi, lettuce, mushrooms, potatoes, runner beans, squash, sweetcorn, tomatoes, turnips
Apples, apricots, blackberries, blackcurrants, blueberries, figs, loganberries, mulberries, nectarines, passion fruit, peaches, pears, plums, raspberries, redcurrants, tayberries, whitecurrants

October
Aubergines, beetroot, Brussels sprouts, carrots, cauliflower, celeriac, celery, chillies, garlic, kohlrabi, leeks, marrow, mushrooms, onions, pumpkin, swede, squash, sweet potatoes, Swiss chard
Apples, crab apples, damsons, figs, pears, quince

November

Beetroot, broccoli, Brussels sprouts, cabbages, carrots, cauliflower, celeriac, celery, chicory, leeks, onions, parsnips, pumpkin, squash, swede, Swiss chard
Apples, crab apples, forced rhubarb, grapefruit, medlars, oranges, pears, quince, sloes

December

Beetroot, broccoli, Brussels sprouts, cabbages, carrots, cauliflower, celeriac, chicory, leeks, parsnips, swede, Swiss chard, winter greens
Apples, crab apples, cranberries, forced rhubarb, grapefruit, oranges

---

COOKS IN BOOKS

A hardened and shameless tea-drinker who has, for twenty years, diluted his meals with only the infusion of this fascinating plant; whose kettle has scarcely time to cool, who with tea amuses the evening, with tea solaces the midnight, and with tea welcomes the morning.

Dr Samuel Johnson's description of himself in *The Literary Magazine*

OLD PICTURE, NEW CAPTION

Pickwick was unable to hide his disappointment on learning that the steamed treacle pudding was finished for the day.

LITERARY FEASTS

The wedding feast of Camacho in Cervantes' Don Quixote gave rise to the expression 'noces de Camache', meaning an improbably large feast costing a considerable amount of money.

The first thing that met Sancho's eyes was a whole ox spitted on the trunk of an elm and, in the hearth over which it was to roast, there was a fair mountain of wood burning. Six earthen pots were arranged around this blaze... Whole sheep disappeared within them as if they were pigeons. Innumerable skinned hares and fully plucked chickens, hanging on the trees, were soon to be swallowed up in these pots. Birds and game too, of all kinds, were also hanging from the branches so that they were kept cool in the air... There were piles of white loaves, like heaps of wheat in barns. Cheeses, built up like bricks, formed walls and two cauldrons of oil, bigger than dyer's vats, were used for frying pastries, which were lifted out with two sturdy shovels and then plunged into another cauldron of honey standing nearby.

Miguel de Cervantes, *Don Quixote*

QUOTE UNQUOTE

After a good dinner, one can forgive anybody, even one's own relations.
OSCAR WILDE, playwright and poet

CRÈME DE LA CRÈME

The expression *cordon bleu*, the byword for high-class cooking, originated with L'Ordre des Chevaliers du Saint-Esprit, the highest order of knighthood in France, which was created in 1578 by Henri III. These exalted knights wore a medal attached to a blue ribbon and their spectacular feasts became legendary throughout the country. The term, therefore, came to be used to describe outstanding chefs capable of preparing the very best feasts. The cooking school was founded in 1895, 'to promote the worldwide appreciation of gastronomy and to encourage excellence in the culinary arts'. There are now 22 Cordon Bleu schools in 12 countries around the world.

COOKING CONUNDRUMS

You throw away the outside and cook the inside. Then you eat the outside and throw away the inside. What did you eat?
Answer on page 153

SAY IT WITH FOOD

Pigs are a popular subject when it comes to cautionary phrases...
A pig's whisper – very short space of time
Bartholomew pig – a fat person; from the chief attraction of a roasted pig at Bartholomew Fair
He may fetch a flitch of bacon from Dunmow – to enjoy marital harmony
Like a pig in a poke – a blind bargain
Pigs in clover – people with newly acquired money who don't know how to behave now they have it
Pig-headed – stubborn and stupid
Squealing like a stuck pig – shouting with pain
Staring like a stuck pig – with mouth open and eyes wide
To baste your bacon – to strike or scourge, as the bacon was the outside of the pig, so would receive any blows aimed at the unfortunate animal
To bring home the bacon – to earn the family's living, possibly a reference to the sport of catching a greased pig at country fairs
To eat Dunmow bacon – to live in conjugal bliss
To go to pigs and whistles – to be ruined
To make a pig's ear – to mess something up
To make a silk purse out of a sow's ear – to turn something unpromising into a triumph
To pull bacon – to cock a snook
To save one's bacon – to rescue oneself; possibly referring to saving the last of the bacon from the scavenging dogs of the house
When pigs fly – never

CULINARY LEGENDS

Paul Bocuse is the latest in a long family line of French chefs and restaurateurs that dates back to 1765. Born in 1926, he began his career at the age of 16 at a restaurant in Lyon and worked under several chefs before taking over his family's failing restaurant in Collonge in 1959 and saving it from ruin. His trademark has been to refresh the classics of French cuisine, using simpler recipes, market-fresh food and emphasising natural flavours and textures. This lighter style caught on with many younger chefs, and Bocuse has become an indefatigable ambassador of French cuisine, travelling around the world, giving lectures and masterclasses, especially in Japan. While modernising the cuisine, he has lost none of the French love of rich foods; among his creations are black truffle soup, lobster Meursault and a chocolate gâteau.

DANGEROUS FOODS

Bitter almonds contain poisonous prussic acid.

Bitter manioc contains cyanide and is very toxic unless pounded, grated, soaked and heated. In 1981, a water shortage in Mozambique meant that it was not prepared thoroughly and over 1,000 people suffered paralysis after eating it.

Carrots eaten in excess can cause jaundice.

Liver eaten in excess can cause vitamin A overdose and birth defects.

Mochi, a Japanese New Year's food, is traditionally made outdoors by pounding a steamed, glutinous rice with a large wooden mallet until a gummy mass forms. The mochi must be chewed carefully, or it can cause choking when swallowed.

The **Nardoo seeds** used by aboriginals to make cakes are toxic when raw. They were the final meal of explorers Burke and Wills in 1861.

Nutmeg eaten in excess can be hallucinogenic.

Red kidney beans are toxic if inadequately boiled.

Green potatoes are poisonous when raw.

Rhubarb leaves are full of oxalic acid and should never be eaten.

Taro leaves, the leaves of a tropical starchy tuber contain oxalic acid and can only be eaten when well cooked.

WORLD CLASS PORRIDGE

Every year in Carrbridge in Inverness-shire, the villagers uphold the standards of Scottish porridge by holding the Golden Spurtle World Porridge Championships. The prize is awarded to the entrant who makes the best traditional porridge using nothing more than water, oatmeal and salt – although they can choose from pinhead, coarse, medium or fine oatmeal. There is also a Speciality Porridge section for more creative recipes, which can use non-traditional ingredients such as fruit. Entrants must make a pint of porridge for the judges, who award marks for consistency, colour and taste. No equipment is provided, as it is assumed that entrants will bring their own favourite porridge pan and spurtle (stirrer). Pre-soaking is allowed, but oat flakes are forbidden (the oatmeal must be untreated). As well as carrying off the Golden Spurtle Challenge Trophy and the coveted title of World Porridge Making Champion, the winner receives £500 and a weekend for two at a luxury hotel, which includes, presumably, a hearty breakfast.

The menu for Henry IV's coronation dinner, at Westminster in 1399:

First course

Braun en peuerarde	Brawn in a pottage of wine, spices, onions and vinegar
Viaund Ryal	A white soup of almond milk, rice flour, milk and spices
Teste de senglere enarme	Boar's head and tusks
Graund chare	Roasted haunches of meat
Syngnettys	Cygnets
Capoun de haut grece	Larded capons
Fesaunte	Pheasant
Heroun	Heron
Crustade lumbarde	Pie containing custard, bone marrow, dates and prunes
Storeioun, graunt luces	Sturgeon, large pike

Second course

Venyson in furmenty	Venison with wheat boiled in sweetened and spiced milk
Gely	Aspic
Porcelle farce enforce	Stuffed sucking-pig
Pokokkys	Peacocks
Cranys	Cranes
Venyson Roste	Roast venison
Conyng	Grown rabbit
Byttore	Bittern
Pulle endore	Gilded chickens (with flour, egg yolks, ginger and saffron)
Graunt tartez	Tarts containing capons, chicken, duck, game, egg, marrow, dates and spices
Braun fryez	Chopped brawn in batter
Leche lumbarde	Dates cooked in wine, then ground and spiced

Third course

Blaundesorye	White soup (of almond milk, almonds and capon flesh)
Quyncys in comfyte	Preserved quinces
Egretez	Egrets
Curlewys	Curlews
Pertryche	Partridge
Pyionys	Pigeons
Quaylys	Quails
Snytys	Snipe
Smal byrdys	Little birds
Rabettys	Young rabbits
Pome dorreng	Rissoles of pork or beef in sweetened golden batter
Braun blanke leche	Brawn with almond milk and sugar, sliced and eaten cold
Eyroun engele	Eggs in jelly
Frytourys	Pancakes
Doucettys	Cheesecakes
Pety pernaux	Little pies

TABLE MANNERS

In medieval times, dagger-shaped knifes and spoons were being used as cutlery in Europe. But forks had not yet caught on, and food was for the most part eaten with the fingers. This made hygiene somewhat important, especially as dishes were set in the middle of the table for everyone to dip into. A number of etiquette books at the time felt it necessary to recommend that diners avoid putting their fingers into their ears or noses, or scratching their heads or private parts in between forays into the stew. The same writers also felt moved to warn people not to poke around on the central platter looking for the nicest bit of meat, nor to put gnawed bones back in the dish. Instead, they should throw them on the floor, like everyone else.

A CAUTIONARY LIMERICK

> There was a young gourmet of Crediton
> Who took pâté de foie gras and spread it on
> A chocolate biscuit
> He murmured 'I'll risk it'
> His tomb bears the date that he said it on.

Anon

NEW IN STORE

The explosion of expeditions to the New World (the Americas) in the 16th and 17th centuries introduced new flavours to the European table:

beans – kidney, butter and scarlet runner beans, brought back by Columbus
chillies – brought back by Columbus
chocolate – brought back by Cortés
maize – brought back from Cuba by Columbus
Guinea-fowl – brought by Portuguese from West Africa, around 1530
Jerusalem artichokes – discovered by Champlain in Canada in 1603
pineapples – brought back by Columbus; he thought it the most delicious fruit in the world
potatoes – Sir Francis Drake brought the potato back from the Caribbean, where he stopped in 1586
tomatoes – brought back from Mexico in 1519 by Cortés
turkey – brought back from Mexico around 1523 by Levantine or Turkish merchants, hence its name (its Mexican name was *uexolotl*)

The New World also gave us avocados, haricot beans, French beans, peanuts, vanilla, red peppers, green peppers and tapioca.

QUOTE UNQUOTE

Bouillabaisse is only good because cooked by the French, who, if they cared to try, could produce an excellent and nutritious substitute out of cigar stumps and empty matchboxes.
NORMAN DOUGLAS, novelist

HONEY TROUBLE

Lovers of honey have long been troubled by the phenomenon that if you spread honey onto a piece of unbuttered toast, the toast becomes concave. The reason is simple. Bread is approximately 40% water, while honey is a concentrated solution made up of around 80% sugars. Osmosis draws water out of the bread and into the honey, causing the bread to become concave. Fortunately the solution is also simple – a thin layer of butter or margarine will protect the toast from this distressing effect.

FULL OF BEANS

Beans are one of the world's oldest foods. They're full of protein, vitamins, minerals, carbohydrates and fibre, they're low in fat and salt, contain no cholesterol, can be stored for a long time and they're cheap. Try a new flavour today:

black beans: black-skinned kidney beans with white flesh, common in Latin America

black-eyed peas: small and creamy white with a black spot, easily digestible

borlotti beans: long pale pink or beige Italian beans, creamy and slightly sweet

butter beans: flat, white beans, soft floury texture

cannellini beans: small white kidney beans

flageolet beans: delicate pale green or white, gourmet kidney beans

Greek beans: large flat beans with no skin, good for puréeing

large white kidney beans: one of the largest beans, flat, white and buttery, much used in Spain and France

pinto beans: small kidney bean with pink, speckled skin, used in south-west USA and Latin America

red kidney beans: one of the most familiar beans, used in chilli con carne

small white haricot (navy) beans: typically used in French cassoulet and by Mr Heinz for his baked beans in tomato sauce

SAY IT WITH FOOD

As well as eggheads, bad eggs and too many eggs in one basket, there are plenty more eggy exhortations:

A duck's egg
No score in cricket, as in 'out for a duck'

As sure as eggs is eggs
Thought to be a corruption of a mathematical formula (as sure as x = x)

Curate's egg
Good in parts, from a Punch cartoon showing a nervous young curate eating breakfast with a bishop. When asked how his poorly cooked egg tasted, he replies anxiously: 'Parts of it are excellent!'

I have eggs on the spit
I am too busy to do anything else

To crush in the egg
To stop something before it has started

Show him an egg and the air is full of feathers
A variation on counting one's chickens before they're hatched

The mundane egg
Some early civilisations believed the world was egg shaped and a bird was often depicted laying 'the mundane egg', the fledgling world, on a primordial sea

There is reason for roasting egg
There is always a reason why something is done in a certain way

Like as two eggs
Identical

To take eggs for money
To be imposed upon, ie do something you don't really want to do

Egg-trot
A cautious trotting pace, like that of a person carrying eggs to market

A hen on a hot griddle
Scottish equivalent of a cat on a hot tin roof, a restless person

TIS AN ILL WIND

According to Reay Tannahill's *Food in History*, the aspect of dining etiquette that has attracted the most comment throughout history is that of breaking wind. In China, farting in public was specifically banned as long ago as the 6th century BC. In India 400 years later, etiquette regarding meeting the king forbade anyone to 'indulge in loud laughter where there is no joke, nor break wind'. Emperor Claudius took a different line, allowing his fellow diners to release their intestinal gases, as he feared that restraining the impulse might do some damage – which suggests that until then it had indeed been banned.

COOKING CONUNDRUMS

My first is in dill but never in sage
My second's in apple and also greengage
My third is in bread but never in butter
My fourth is in foil but never in cutter
My fifth is in sausage but never in roll
My whole serves your dinner, straight from the bowl
What am I?
Answer on page 153

OLD PICTURE, NEW CAPTION

When Cook was trying out a new recipe, Albert couldn't always bring himself to look into the tureen.

SUMPTUARY LAWS

In times of feasting, governments have occasionally resorted to restricting their citizens from overeating. In ancient Rome, the authorities forbade the eating of very young animals and the slaughter of selected species. They banned displays of luxury and commanded that everyone eat with their doors open, to make it easier for the laws to be enforced. The same tactic was tried in France during the Ancien Regime, when citizens were no longer allowed to serve more than eight courses at dinner, which suggests that the laws were sorely needed.

EDIBLE PLAYS

An Absolute Turkey – Georges Feydeau
Bitter Sweet – Noel Coward
The Cherry Orchard – Anton Chekhov
Chicken Soup with Barley – Arnold Wesker
Chips with Everything – Arnold Wesker
The Cocktail Party – TS Eliot
The Curse of the Starving Class – Sam Shepard
A Day in the Death of Joe Egg – Peter Nichols
Duck Variations – David Mamet
The Farm – David Storey
The Gingerbread Lady – Neil Simon
The Grain of Mustard Seed – Harold Harwood
Icecream – Caryl Churchill
Individual Fruit Pies – Mike Leigh
The Kitchen – Arnold Wesker
The Last Bread – HE Bates
Lettice and Lovage– Peter Shaffer
The Long Christmas Dinner – Thornton Wilder
Nuts in May – Mike Leigh
Salt of the Earth – John Godber
Separate Tables – Terence Rattigan
Table Manners – Alan Ayckbourn
Under Milk Wood – Dylan Thomas
What the Butler Saw – Joe Orton
The Wild Duck – Henrik Ibsen

LITERARY FEASTS

It is after lunch and I shall now describe the house. For lunch, I may say, I ate and greatly enjoyed the following: anchovy paste on hot buttered toast, then baked beans and kidney beans with chopped celery, tomatoes, lemon juice and olive oil. (Really good olive oil is essential, the kind with a taste, I have brought a supply from London.) Green peppers would have been a happy addition only the village shop (about two miles pleasant walk) could not provide them... Then bananas and cream with white sugar. Bananas should be cut, never mashed, and the cream should be thin. Then hard water biscuits with New Zealand butter and Wensleydale cheese. Of course I never touch foreign cheeses. Our cheeses are the best in the world. With this feast I drank most of a bottle of Muscadet out of my modest 'cellar'. I ate and drank slowly as one should (cook fast, eat slow) and without distractions (thank heavens) conversation or reading. Indeed eating is so pleasant that one should even try to suppress thought.

Iris Murdoch, *The Sea, The Sea*

EXPERT ADVICE

How to tell if an egg is fresh

Once an egg has been laid, it has a limited shelf life, as the egg white and yolk slowly break down inside the shell. As this happens, air accumulates within the shell, so the older the egg, the more air is inside it. To test if an egg is fresh, place it in a deep bowl of water. If it lies on the bottom, it is fresh. If it stands on one end and bobs on the bottom of the bowl, it is a little older but still edible, ideal for scrambling or hard-boiling. If the whole egg floats to the surface, it is probably rotten.

I'LL HAVE MINE OVER EASY

For those unfamiliar with American English, here's a quick guide to make sure you don't go hungry:

aubergine – eggplant
biscuit – cookie
candyfloss – cotton candy
chick pea – garbanzo bean
chips – French fries
coriander – cilantro (the fresh herb)
cos lettuce – romaine lettuce
courgette – zucchini
crisps – chips
double cream – whipping cream
filter coffee – drip coffee
hot dog – weenie/wiener
ice lolly – Popsicle
icing sugar – powdered sugar
jam – jelly
jelly – jello
mange tout – snow pea
minced meat – ground meat
offal – variety meat
okra – gumbo
peppers – bell peppers
rocket – arugula
rosé wine – blush wine
sorbet – sherbet
spring onions – scallions
swede – rutabaga
sweet potato – yam
sweets – candy
Swiss roll – jelly roll
wholemeal biscuit – Graham cracker

BULKING UP

In the 19th century, as the population grew and the food industry had to keep pace, unscrupulous manufacturers and traders took to bulking up or enhancing their product with other less expensive ingredients:

Boiled sweets were coloured with salts of copper and lead (poisonous)

Bread was often (unsafely) whitened with alum

China tea was mixed with thorn leaves coloured with verdigris (poisonous)

Coffee was diluted with ground chicory or acorns

Cocoa was diluted with brick dust

Gloucester cheese owed its red rind to a red lead colouring (poisonous)

Pepper was bulked out with mustard husks, pea flour and dust swept up from the floor

Pickles were made green with copper (poisonous)

Tea leaves were often mixed with dried ash leaves; merchants also took used tea leaves, dried them, coloured them black with lead (poisonous) and resold them

Wine was flavoured with bitter almonds, which contained prussic acid (poisonous)

QUOTE UNQUOTE

Some cook, some do not cook, some things can not be altered.
EZRA POUND, US poet

READ THE LABEL

Helpful advice found on food packaging...

On a bag of Fritos: You could be a winner! No purchase necessary. Details inside.

On Swanson frozen dinners: Serving suggestion: Defrost.

On Tesco's tiramisu dessert (printed on bottom): Do not turn upside down.

On Marks & Spencer Bread Pudding: Product will be hot after heating.

On Salisbury's peanuts: Warning: Contains nuts.

On an American Airlines packet of nuts: Instructions: Open packet. Eat nuts.

On a Japanese food processor: Not to be used for the other use.

Caviar has long been the badge of upmarket dining, and still divides gourmets the world over. Given that caviar is merely fish eggs – albeit rare fish eggs – it is often denounced as being over-rated. Caviar has been revered for centuries, in places such as ancient Egypt, Greece, Persia and Rome. The huge price is the result of the difficulty of obtaining the right kind of sturgeon, which should be beluga, ossetra, sevruga. For years the majority of caviar has come from the Black Sea and the Caspian Sea, but Iranian caviar is exceptionally good and is gaining ground fast. Good caviar should be not too salty, and should smell like fresh salt water. It should have an unbroken glistening, thin outer membrane with distinct individual roe or eggs, and should be eaten from a horn spoon, so it is not tainted with the taste of metal.

Truffles are edible subterranean mushrooms that are hard to find, and therefore a much sought-after delicacy. Pungent tasting and rich-smelling, these fungi are roundish and semi-hard, and look like a brown, wrinkled root vegetable. Trained truffling pigs or dogs are used to find them, as only they can smell the pungent scent above ground, and this somewhat archaic method of hunting and gathering only adds to the mystique – and to the price.

Saffron strands are the stamens of the saffron crocus, which are harvested, dried and then used in cooking. It is mainly grown in Spain and India, though was grown in the UK from the 15th to 18th century. Its considerable cost is because it is hard to obtain; to produce saffron, the stamens must be individually extracted, not an easy job considering the tiny size of the plant. To produce a pound of saffron you would need to individually hand-treat 25,000 stamens and each crocus provides only three stamens, which explains its excessive cost.

YOU NEVER CAN TELL

Jerome Irving Rodale, the founding father of the organic food movement, creator of *Organic Farming and Gardening* magazine, and founder of Rodale Press, a major publishing corporation, died while discussing the benefits of organic foods on a TV chat show.

Rodale was 72 when he appeared on the *Dick Cavett Show* in January 1971. Part way through the interview, he dropped dead in his chair from a heart attack. He had claimed 'I'm going to live to be 100 unless I'm run down by a sugar-crazed taxi driver.' The show was never aired.

MEAT THE NEIGHBOURS

Sawney Bean (c. 1400) plumbed the depths of human depravity to an extent not seen before or since. With a female partner, he took up residence in a seaside cave in Scotland and lived by robbing, murdering and then eating his victims. His family – which grew to include 14 children and 34 grandchildren, all the result of incest – joined in, helping with the murder, dismemberment, pickling and salting of human flesh. If, as often happened, they built up a surplus, they would simply throw any spare limbs into the sea. It was assumed that the Beans had consumed around 1,000 victims before the king himself led a search to hunt down the culprits. The entire family was seized and executed without trial.

FIRST PAST THE POST

Tasty-sounding winners of some of Britain's key horse races:

1777	Bourbon	St Leger
1778	Hollandaise	St Leger
1785	Trifle	Oaks
1796	Ambrosio	St Leger
1808	Morel	Oaks
1837	Mango	St Leger
1855	Saucebox	St Leger
1822	Pastille	Oaks
1843	Poison	Oaks
1854	Mincemeat	Oaks
1856	Mince Pie	Oaks
1868	The Lamb	Grand National
1871	The Lamb	Grand National
1882	Dutch Oven	St Leger
1893	Mrs Butterwick	Oaks
1896	Persimmon	St Leger and Derby
1905	Cherry Lass	Oaks
1906	Spearmint	Derby
1916	Vermouth	Grand National
1924	Salmon-Trout	St Leger
1931	Sandwich	St Leger
1959	Oxo	Grand National
1966	Sodium	St Leger
1973	Red Rum	Grand National
1974	Red Rum	Grand National
1975	L'Escargot	Grand National
1977	Red Rum	Grand National

A BRIEF HISTORY OF CHOCOLATE

• Chocolate was first consumed by the Aztecs and their predecessors in the south Americas as a bitter, savoury drink made by roasting and pounding the cocoa beans, and adding flavourings such as chilli and pepper. The Aztec word for chocolate was *xocolatl*, meaning 'bitter water'.

• The cocoa tree was so valuable that the seeds were used as currency. A slave cost around 100 cocoa beans, and the services of a 'public woman' cost 10 cocoa beans – the same price as a rabbit.

• Columbus 'discovered' the cocoa bean in 1502, but when he took it home to King Ferdinand, the King showed no interest. The discovery is credited instead to the Spanish conquistador Hérnando Cortés. After landing in Mexico in 1519, he took the cocoa bean back to Spain, where vanilla and sugar (also new to Spain) were added to the bitter drink.

• The botanist Linnaeus named the cocoa tree *Theobroma cacao*, meaning 'food of the gods'. The cocoa bean includes theobromine, a very mild stimulant that triggers the release of endorphins in the brain, which in turn create feelings of euphoria, particularly of love and arousal. Casanova recommended a cup of hot chocolate as a 'restorative', and preferred it to champagne.

• When Anne of Spain married Louis XIII of France in 1651, she brought her own chocolate with her, and a maid, La Molina, whose sole task was to prepare it.

• Pope Pius V thought hot chocolate so disgusting that there was no need to ban it during Lent.

• In mid-17th century Spain, the Bishop of Chiapa was allegedly poisoned by a cup of hot cocoa after he tried to ban women from drinking hot chocolate in church.

• Chocolate arrived in England in the 1650s and was served in coffee-houses as well as in chocolate houses such as Whites. In an effort to prevent the rowdy behaviour and gambling that these places encouraged, Charles II tried to suppress the coffee-houses in a proclamation in 1675, but it was largely ignored.

• Sir Hans Sloane, physician to Queen Anne and Samuel Pepys, is credited with first adding milk rather than water to hot chocolate. He sold his recipe to an apothecary, and it later passed into the hands of the Cadbury brothers.

• Solid chocolate was first created in 1819 by Frenchman Francois-Louis Cailler.

• In 1847, Fry's became the first British company to make solid chocolate bars for eating, having discovered independently of Cailler how to solidify the mixture.

• Cadbury's supplied 1,500lbs chocolate to Scott's expedition to the Antarctic on his discovery tour in 1901-1904.

• Quality Street chocolates, launched in 1936, were named after a play by JM Barrie.

• Milton Snavely Hershey, the American confectionery millionaire, was the inspiration for Roald Dahl's *Willy Wonka*.

LITERARY FEASTS

And suddenly the memory revealed itself. The taste was that of the little piece of Madeleine which on Sunday mornings at Combray (because on those mornings I did not go out before Mass), when I went to say good morning to her in her bedroom, my Aunt Leonie used to give me, dipping it first in her own cup of tea or tisane.

Marcel Proust, *A La Récherche du Temps Perdu*

SAY IT WITH FOOD

A little pot is soon hot – a small person is easily riled

Bachelor's fare – bread, cheese and kisses

Baker's knee – knock-knees (because of the baker's habit of standing all day)

Bread and circuses – free food and entertainment

Cry barley – call a truce (barley is a corruption of 'parley' and was a cry for truce in a rough game)

Don't roast your coffee beans in the marketplace – don't tell your secrets to a stranger

Fiddler's pay – meat, drink and money

Fingers were made before forks – don't stand on ceremony

Ginger group – a small group designed to spice up the apathetic majority, usually in politics

He eats no fish – someone who is honest and trustworthy (used in Elizabeth I's time, as protestants refused to adopt the Roman Catholic custom of eating fish on a Friday)

Hungry dogs will eat dirty pudding – a hungry person will eat anything

It is time to lay our nuts aside – time to leave off childish pursuits and become adults

Measure other people's corn by one's own bushel – judge others using yourself as the standard

Men of the same kidney – of the same disposition (kidneys were thought to be the seat of affection)

Soft (or fair) words butter no parsnips – mere words will not get us fed

So that accounts for the milk in the coconut – said when the cause of something becomes apparent

To cabbage – to pilfer

To have an ostrich stomach – to be able to digest anything

To make chalk of one and cheese of the other – to favour one over the other

To take pepper in the nose – to take offence

Tis an old rat that won't eat cheese – only a very wise or experienced person won't take a juicy bait

With an eye to the loaves and fishes – with an eye on the material rewards

Temperature, in degrees fahrenheit, at which hot food should be kept 145

FOUR AND TWENTY BLACKBIRDS
BAKED IN A PIE

Cooks in wealthy households in the late Middle Ages spent a lot of time on presentation, creating stunning centrepieces and decorative food to amuse the diners. Occasionally their dishes were designed to be more entertaining than edible. This recipe, roughly translated, is one example:

Make the coffin [piecrust] of a great pie. In the bottom make a hole as big as your fist, or bigger if you will. Let the sides of the coffin be some-what higher than ordinary pies. Which done, put it full of flour and bake it, and being baked, open the hole in the bottom and take out the flour. Then [taking] a pie of the bigness of the hole in the bottom of the coffin, you shall put it into the coffin, and put into the coffin around the pie as many small live birds as the empty coffin will hold... And this is to be done at such time as you send the pie to the table, and set before the guests: where, uncovering or cutting up the great lid of the pie, all the birds will fly out, which is to delight and pleasure show to the company. And that they be not altogether mocked, you shall cut open the small pie.

WHAT'S FOR DINNER, DARLING?

• Susan Barber killed her husband by putting weedkiller in his steak and kidney pie. She was jailed for life in 1982.

• Florence Maybrick killed her husband with arsenic after he beat her for taking a lover (although he had a mistress). She served 15 years of a life-sentence and died in 1941.

• Madeleine Smith poisoned her lover by putting arsenic in his hot chocolate when he broke off their affair. She was acquitted when the defence showed that he was a seducer and a habitual user of arsenic. Smith died in 1928, aged 93.

• Dr Hawley Crippen poisoned his overbearing wife, so he could be with his lover. He was hanged in 1910.

• Adelaide Bartlett was accused in 1886 of poisoning her husband with chloroform after he encouraged her relationship with another man, left her everything in his will, and made her lover the executor. She was acquitted when no one could work out how she'd got him to swallow the chloroform (it burns the throat).

• Mary Ann Cotton killed an unspecified number of people (30 or more) with arsenic, including her second husband, two stepsons and two of her lovers. She was hanged in 1873.

• Margaret Fernseed, prostitute and brothel-keeper, was convicted of the murder of her husband, after it was noted (on finding his dead body) that she had at one time tried to poison him. She was hanged in 1608.

Published during World War II, *Come Into the Garden, Cook* by Constance Spry urged those on the home front to venture into their gardens and to grow their own food. Her no-nonsense tone and practical abilities – she had an extensive kitchen garden of her own – makes for an inspiring book, whose principles are still relevant today.

Thinking of Italy brings me to the subject of garlic. Hypersensitive nostrils are apt to quiver disapproval at the very mention of garlic. If it's a matter of enduring the smell of it in the Paris underground, I am with them, but not when cookery is in question. Take, for instance, the recipe for white haricots on page 73. Garlic here is an indispensable ingredient, and yet I doubt whether a normally sensitive palate could single out its flavour in the finished dish. Tomato sauces call for its use, and such meat dishes as navarin of mutton. For those who frankly like garlic there is all the range of salads in which subtly to employ it. For those who unblushingly enjoy it, I will tell how I ate it once in America. Those who find the taste vulgar had best skip the following paragraphs.

One Sunday I found myself for a single day in a town in Oregon. I spent the morning reading the papers. These gave me a strange disoriented feeling – I think it must have been the display advertisements of the town's churches, which set out in good commercial style the merits and benefits on offer, headed in most cases by a photograph of the incumbent. I felt a million miles from home. Then I went to a dinner party, and had the same sensation I used to have long ago at the transformation scene in the pantomime and Europe seemed suddenly close at hand again. Lovely rooms, priceless pictures, elegant women in Paris clothes, cosmopolitan food touching perfection – in no city have I eaten more exquisite food. At the moment when we were eating a superlative salad, a long loaf was brought in, very light in texture – as indeed is most American bread – hot, crisp and sliced. Between each slice and on all sides fresh butter had been thickly spread and the loaf reheated in the oven. The butter had been lightly flavoured with garlic.

I will admit that we repaired afterwards to bathrooms of such perfection as are not to be found in Europe, and dealt faithfully with a few mouthwashes, but no one seemed inhibited or worried. I believe I was the only one who wondered if, at a later gathering, we should steal on the air like a pale blue sensation.

QUOTE UNQUOTE

Poets have been mysteriously silent on the subject of cheese.
GK CHESTERTON, author

NO FOOD, IT'S FRIDAY

The tradition of fasting was first recorded around the 2nd century, and was usually practised as a way of martyring oneself when persecuted. It evolved into a sign of holiness (and of self-control, important given what happened in the Garden of Eden), and was one way to achieve perfection and purity. At first the practice was voluntary, but by the 6th century the Church had made it compulsory. Wednesdays and Fridays were fast days, and one was expected to fast before baptism and during any period of penance. The Easter fast of Lent, originally four days long, gradually stretched into 40 days of self-denial. However for most people, fasting meant abstaining from certain foods rather than eating nothing at all. Still, when fast days came to include every Wednesday, Friday and Sunday as well as Lent, even that became a bit trying. The ordinary man, if he dared, could risk a little discreet cheating, but it was no small risk – until the mid-1500s, it was technically possible to be hanged for eating meat on a Friday. The rules were occasionally relaxed as the Church went through phases of allowing dairy foods, eggs and fish during fasts, which made Lent the most prosperous time of year for the salted fish merchants. But sooner or later there would be a fit of piety and everyone would be back on bread and vegetables.

QUOTE UNQUOTE

Chemically speaking, chocolate really is the world's perfect food.
MICHAEL LEVINE, nutrition researcher

OSBERT'S MARVELLOUS EGG

Sir George Reresby Sitwell (1860-1943), father of the literary trio Osbert, Sacheverell and Edith, was a keen medievalist and inventor and one of England's more entertaining eccentrics. His several sitting rooms were filled with boxes containing notes on monographs yet to be written, such as 'Acorns as an Article of Medieval Diet' and 'My Inventions'. One of these inventions was the Sitwell Egg. Devised as a nourishing and easily transportable meal for travellers, it comprised a 'yolk' of smoked meat and a 'white' of compressed rice contained within a synthetic shell. He presented it to Gordon Selfridge, the founder of Selfridges, but as nothing more was heard of it, we must assume that Mr Selfridge was unimpressed. Which is surprising, given that one of Sir George's rules of life was that he should never be contradicted, as it interfered with the functioning of his gastric juices, and he erected a sign to that effect at his home, Renishaw Hall in Derbyshire, to warn off argumentative visitors.

A SHORT HISTORY OF TEA

Given that tea is so firmly associated with England, it is surprising to learn that we were one of the last European countries to taste it. Tea first reached Holland in 1610 and spread to neighbouring countries decades before we got so much as a sniff. The French adopted it with great enthusiasm, although once the novelty had worn off, they returned to their first love, coffee. The first public sale of tea in England was in 1657 and it quickly replaced ale as the national drink, which had a helpful effect on national sobriety. Its popularity was encouraged by Catherine of Braganza, who, when she married Charles II in 1662, brought with her from Portugal a love of tea – and whatever was popular at court tended to become fashionable.

In 1699, England was taking delivery of 40,000lbs; by 1790, we were consuming 18 million lbs of tea a year. But like most popular foodstuffs, it became a target for taxation, attracting a duty from the moment it arrived. At first this was only around a shilling a pound (to pay for the Battle of the Boyne) but by 1773, tax accounted for 64% of its price.

High taxes, of course, encouraged smuggling and the tea tax was constantly being reduced to put the smugglers out of business then raised again when the government ran out of money. Ironically it was the Boston Tea Party that put tea taxes in the UK up to their all-time high of 119% in 1784; the money was needed to quell the American revolution. But soon after, the tax was cut drastically, to end the smuggling once and for all, and tea was able to take its rightful place as the nation's favourite drink.

LITERARY FEASTS

'I simply cannot understand people who are vegetarians,' said the Countess, banging vigorously at a snipe's skull with her fork so that she might crack it and get to the brain. 'Henri once tried to be a vegetarian. Would you believe it? But I couldn't endure it. "Henri," I said to him, "this must stop. We have enough food in the larder to feed an army, and I can't eat it single-handed." Imagine, my dear, I had just ordered two dozen hares. "Henri," I said, "you will have to give up this foolish fad." '

It struck me that Henri, although obviously a bit of a trial as a husband, had nevertheless led a very frustrated existence.

Gerald Durrell, *Birds, Beasts and Relatives*

COOKING CONUNDRUMS

My first is in soup and also in spoon • My second's in honey and also in moon • My third is in whiting but never in sprat • My fourth is in marrow but never in fat • My fifth is in gin but never in rye • My whole is quite complex and potent, you'll cry • What am I?

Answer on page 153

RECIPE FOR WONKA-VITE

Take a block of finest chocolate weighing one ton (or 20 sackfuls of broken chocolate whichever is the easier). Place chocolate in very large cauldron and melt over red-hot furnace. When melted, lower the heat slightly so as not to burn the chocolate, but keep it boiling. Now add the following, in precisely the order given, stirring well all the time and allowing each item to dissolve before adding the next:

The hoof of a manticore
The trunk (and the suitcase) of an elephant
The yolks of three eggs from a whiffle-bird
A wart from a wart-hog
The horn of a cow (it must be a loud horn)
The front tail of a cockatrice
Six ounces of sprunge from a young slimescraper
Two hairs (and one rabbit) from the head of a hippocampus
The beak of a red-breasted wilbatross
A corn from the toe of a unicorn
The four tentacles of a quadropus
The hip (and the po and the pot) of a hippopotamus
The snout of a proghopper
A mole from a mole
The hide (and the seek) of a spotted whangdoodle
The whites of 12 eggs from a tree-squeak
The three feet of a snozzwanger (if you can't get three feet, one yard will do)
The square-root of a south American abacus
The fangs of a viper (it must be a vindscreen viper)
The chest (and the drawers) of a wild grout

When all the above are thoroughly dissolved, boil for a further 27 days but do not stir. At the end of this time, all liquid will have evaporated and there will be left in the bottom of the cauldron only a hard brown lump about the size of a football. Break this open with a hammer and in the very centre of it you will find a small round pill. This pill is WONKA-VITE.

Roald Dahl, *Charlie and the Great Glass Elevator*

DURING THE COMPILATION OF THIS BOOK, THE COMPANION TEAM...

Ate 455 hot dinners

Counted the contents of 10 tubes of Smarties (and picked out all the blue ones)

Shopped at four different farmers' markets

Watched seven TV cookery shows

Burned 14 slices of toast (but still ate six of them)

Smuggled one jar of crunchy peanut butter from Boston to London

Ate four slices of birthday cake

Threw five dinner parties

Found three items at the back of the fridge that were no longer identifiable

Tried 10 new recipes, nine quite successfully

Left one bag of groceries under the seat on the Number 12 bus

Baked two cakes (both chocolate)

Drank a lot more coffee than was good for them

Please note that although every effort has been made to ensure accuracy in this book, the above statistics may be the result of over-cooked minds.

There is no love sincerer than the love of food.

George Bernard Shaw

The answers. As if you needed them.

P10.   These are the ingredients for *George's Marvellous Medicine*, from the book by Roald Dahl.

P23.   In *The Merry Wives of Windsor* Bardolph calls Slender a 'Banbury cheese'.

P27.   A snake

P40.   16 inches. Volumes One and 10 remain unmunched.

P47.   Take the fruit from the box marked 'apples and oranges'. If it's an apple, then that box must be the 'apples' box; the box marked 'apples' must contain oranges, and the remaining box both apples and oranges. The opposite is true if you take out an orange.

P52.   People (it's another word for cannibal)

P64.   They're champagne bottle sizes, of which Balthazar (16 bottles) is the largest, a Methuselah contains eight and a Salmanazar 12.

P68.   It is a derivation of the French *fouler*, to crush.

P81.   The *Association Amicale des Amateurs d'Authentiques Andouilletes*, dedicated to andouillettes, a type of pork sausage.

P85.   The full, original name of the Aga stove.

P91.   Lemon and melon

P103. An onion

P109. Hercules, as one of his 12 tasks of penitence.

P115. Seven eggs. The first person bought one half of his eggs plus one half an egg (4 eggs) This left him three eggs. The second person bought one-half of his eggs plus one half an egg, (2 eggs) leaving the man one egg. The last person bought one-half of his eggs plus one-half an egg, (1 egg) leaving no eggs.

P123. An egg

P131. An ear of corn

P138. Ladle

P150. Onion

ACKNOWLEDGEMENTS

We gratefully acknowledge permission to reprint extracts of copyright material in this book from the following authors, publishers and executors:

Extract from *It Must've Been Something I Ate* by Jeffrey Steingarten by kind permission of Random House Inc.

Extract from *Good Morning, Bill* by PG Wodehouse by kind permission of A P Watt Ltd on behalf of the Trustees of the Wodehouse Estate.

Extract from *Two Fat Ladies* by Clarissa Dickson-Wright and Jennifer Paterson published by Ebury. Used by permission of The Random House Group Limited.

Extract from *The Second Sex* by Simone de Beauvoir published by Jonathan Cape/Vintage. Used by permission of The Random House Group Limited.

Extract from *Lady Addle At Home* by Mary Dunn by kind permission of Mrs Jane Sawyer.

Extract from *Drinking the Rain* by Alix Kates Shulman by kind permission of Bloomsbury Publishing Plc.

Extract from *How To Eat* by Nigella Lawson published by Chatto & Windus. Used by permission of The Random House Group Limited.

Extract from *The Sea, The Sea* by Iris Murdoch published by Chatto & Windus. Used by permission of The Random House Group Limited.

Extract from *The Wind in the Willows* by Kenneth Grahame by kind permission of Curtis Brown Group Ltd.

Extract from *Clementine in the Kitchen* by Samuel Chamberlain. Reprinted by permission of David R Godine, Publisher, Inc. Copyright (c) 1988 by Narcisse Chamberlain and Stephanie Chamberlain.

Extract from *The Sword in the Stone* by TH White by kind permission of David Higham Associates Limited.

Extract from *Down With Skool!* © Geoffrey Willans and Ronald Searle 1958. Reproduced by kind permission of The Estate of Geoffrey Willans, Ronald Searle and The Sayle Literary Agency.

Temperature, in degrees centigrade, at which sugar syrup is boiled to make 155 *hard toffee*

BIBLIOGRAPHY

The A-Z of Almost Everything, Trevor Montague

The Atlas of Food, Erik Millstone and Tim Lang

Brewer's Rogues, Villains and Eccentrics,
William Donaldson

Brewer's Phrase and Fable

The Chocolate Book, Helge Rubinstein

The Devil's Cup, Stewart Lee Allen

Feast: A History of Grand Eating, Roy Strong

Food, Clarissa Dickson-Wright

Food: An Oxford Anthology, Brigid Allen

Food in History, Reay Tannahill

The Good Web Guide: Food, Jenni Muir

A History of Britain, Simon Schama

Hungry for You, Joan Smith

In The Devil's Garden, Stewart Lee Allen

It Must've Been Something I Ate, Jeffrey Steingarten

Larousse Gastronomique

Leith's Techniques Bible, Susan Spaull and
Lucinda Bruce-Gardyne

The Little Food Book, Craig Sams

Food: A History, Felipe Fernández-Armesto

The Oxford Companion to the English Language,
Tom McArthur

The Physiology of Taste, Jean Anthelme Brillat-Savarin

A Social History of England, Asa Briggs

Superfoods, Michael Van Straten

The Top Ten of Everything 2004, Russell Ash

The Victory Cookbook, Marguerite Patten

ABOUT THE SOIL ASSOCIATION

The Soil Association was founded in 1946 by Lady Eve Balfour, bringing together farmers, scientists and nutritionists concerned about the impact of intensive farming practices on the environment, food quality and health.

Fifty years on we have become one of the UK's most respected environmental groups, a not-for-profit membership organisation and charity playing a crucial role in the transformation of attitudes to food and farming in the UK and internationally. We are a leading voice among those challenging the industrialisation of agriculture, which we believe has contributed not only to degradation of the countryside but also to increases in diet-related illness, the mistreatment of animals and the betrayal of public trust in food. We work with the public, policy makers, farmers, growers, food processors and retailers to bring about change by creating a growing body of public opinion that understands the links between farming practice and food, and between plant, animal, human and environmental health.

Our work includes:
• Lobbying policy makers
• Raising public awareness
• Educating young people
• Promoting local food
• Advising and representing organic farmers
• Setting organic standards
• Inspecting and certifying farms and organic businesses.

For more information about organic food and farming visit our web site at **www.soilassociation.org**. Or if you would like to join us in our campaign to help build an organic future for our countryside and make organic food and drink accessible to everyone, call **0117 914 2447** today.

Registered charity number 206862

OTHER TITLES AVAILABLE IN THE SERIES

THE GARDENER'S COMPANION
For anyone who has ever put on a pair of gloves, picked up a spade and gone out into a garden in search of flowers, beauty and inspiration. Whether you're a gardener or a garden lover, a veggie planter or an orchid-painter, *The Gardener's Companion* is the perfect pocket filler.
160pp. 2004. ISBN 1-86105-771-7

THE TRAVELLER'S COMPANION
For anyone who's ever stared at a distant plane, wondered where it's going, and spent the rest of the day dreaming of faraway lands and ignoring everything and everyone else. Discover the world from your armchair as you dip into the history and mystery of international travel.
160pp. 2004. ISBN 1-86105-773-3

THE WILDLIFE COMPANION
For anyone who ever heard a bird sing, watched a moth flutter against the light, or ambled through a bluebell wood, and wondered, just momentarily, how such a diverse and beautiful natural world could possibly have come about.
160pp. 2004. ISBN 1-86105-770-9

AND COMING SOON...

THE LITERARY COMPANION 1-86105-798-9

THE LONDON COMPANION 1-86105-799-7

THE MOVIE-GOER'S COMPANION 1-86105-797-0

THE POLITICS COMPANION 1-86105-796-2